2-MINUTE WARNING

Time to Fight for What Matters Most

CHRIS AVILA

2-MINUTE WARNING
Time to Fight for What Matters Most

by Chris Avila

Unless otherwise noted, all scriptures referenced are taken from the *New King James Version* (NKJV) of the Bible. Public domain.

Prepared for printing by Blaze Publishing House

Assisted by Kent Booth

Cover Design by Laura-Lee Booth withBlaze Media House
www.blazemediahouse.com

Printed in the United States.

ISBN-13 (Paperback): 978-0-578-91683-5

What people are saying about Chris Avila . . .

"Chris has an undeniable passion to see people find Jesus and grow in their personal relationship with Him. For decades, Chris has faithfully served the local church and the mission field of 'sports and entertainment.' Chris has given his life to advance the Kingdom, and he is uniquely qualified to minister to professional athletes, as well as everyone desiring to live for God and make their life count. This book will impact and encourage you!"

Landon Schott, Senior Lead Pastor
Mercy Culture Church - Fort Worth, TX

"Chris Avila is a man fully committed to Jesus, his family and to this generation. He has dedicated his life, to see students and athletes break free from the lies and traps of the culture and live out their true identity. This is a crucial moment in our history, and I believe wholeheartedly that God desires to use young people in amazing ways. 2-Minute Warning is a powerful expression of God's heart to aspiring leaders. If you are serious about your life's calling and purpose, this book gives the wisdom and encouragement you'll need for the journey."

PJ Vescovi, Writer, Consultant &
Founder of The Qara Mission

To Kristina, Mayah, Aria, and Diego.

You are my world and my why.

ACKNOWLEDGMENTS

Thank you to my wife and best friend, **Kristina.** Your encouragement, love and belief has fueled me to be my best. Love you. To my amazing three kids, **Mayah, Aria, and Diego**. You are Mommy and Daddy's world.

Pastors Landon & Heather Schott - Your leadership and friendship has impacted us eternally. Your obedience to HIM is a big part this book is here. Thank you.

Mercy Culture Church - Fort Worth, TX - The best church family in the world! Thanks to everyone who celebrated with me and gave to this project. You make it easy to encounter God weekly!

Thank you to these amazing families who have a huge stake in this book and all who will be impacted:

Clay & Lindsay Ingram

David Ybarra

Coach Nathan & Rachel Butler

Jeff Toon & Family

Dave & Patricia Rollins

Andy & Tabitha Cromer

Mike & Lindsay Reiling

Frank Aswad & Family

Jennifer Alex

Kevin & Nicole Jaisen

Julio & Michelle Orozco

Chip & Laury Roop

Brad & Kim Lambert

PJ & Emily Vescovi

To my friends who helped contribute their stories and journeys:

Robert & Casey Guerrero

Bob & Diana Santos

Mario Serrano & Family

Justin Forsett

Kenyon Coleman

Lindsay Rorick

Ervin Wilson

To all my amazing teammates with **Fellowship of Christian Athletes** - You're the best.

To my family:

Monica Quintero - Thanks, Sis, for believing in me. Love you.

Steve & April Vargas - Love you guys, honored you'd invest in this project.

To my amazing team who helped build this book . . . literally:

Brooke West - Your creativity and gifting with my branding is bar none. You're stuck with me now.

Kent & Laura-Lee Booth - My amazing publishers who helped this dream come true. Thank you for pouring everything into this project.

David Fraga - My marketing guru, you are a brilliant entrepreneur. Grateful for you.

CONTENTS

FOREWORD

By LaMorris Crawford

We all know what happens when the two-minute warning hits the game clock. When the referee comes and motions his hands while uttering, "This is the two-minute warning," especially in the fourth quarter, our hearts are pumping out of our chests. Teams have designated designed plays for the moment. They have specific personnel and have every conceivable circumstance outlined in their playbooks. The ultimate goal is to score. Whether that is a touchdown or a field goal, the team wants to win. The success of any two-minute drill is determined by how the team practiced. Practice is the space where preparation is taught and learned. All athletes must learn to prepare for game-time scenarios. Like in a game, this is also true in the life of any athlete. Many athletes live in the two-minute warning zone in their lives. Athletes at all levels have pressures they are facing. Family, friends, finances, performance, and academics—just to name a few. This is where *2-Minute*

Warning: Time to Fight for What Matters Most, written by my good friend Chris Avila, comes in. Chris has written the playbook needed to help athletes of all ages navigate the tenses of life. He has served as a chaplain to athletes at every level from middle school, high school, college, and even the pro level. He has witnessed time and time again the pitfalls that many athletes fall into.

To the teenager who is about to read this book: Take heed. Listen. Re-read and share it with others. The principles that Chris shares are timeless and needed for your generation. The continual compromising of teenagers in America is devastating. The peer pressure, bullying, drinking and partying is tearing your generation apart. But to you who is about to read this book, I am encouraging you to fight for the faith, to hold on to purity and holiness. Chris' words are going to ignite a passion and fire in you for the things of God. You are going to be challenged to meditate on God's Word and keep it as first place in your life. You are going to be challenged to surround yourself with like-minded people. The words in this book will compel you to see the face of Jesus.

Practice is the space where preparation is taught and learned.

- LaMorris Crawford

To the young adult who is about to read this book: Prepare. Focus. Re-read and share it with others. God is raising up a generation of leaders who is unwilling to conform to this world. The Spirit of God is leading and guiding young adults on the path of steadfastness and grit. Chris will dare you to venture into the plan and purpose that God has for your life. You are the leading voice of influence and leadership and this book will be a great resource to help develop you in both areas. Get ready to be challenged in a new and different way. As you apply the principles in this book, you will without a doubt see your life change for the better. You will also see how it will affect those around you.

To the pro athlete who is about to read this book: Take heed. Listen. Pay attention. Learn. Prepare. Focus. Re-read and share with others. I have been serving pro athletes for over 10 years now, while eight of those years being a full-time chaplain for a professional football team. I have walked through some dark valleys with athletes, coaches, and their families.

What I love about this book is how it applies to every level in the life of an athlete. Chris brings insights that I will be able to use to help me walk through life with the athletes I serve. So, if you are in middle school, a teenager, young adult, or pro athlete, *2-Minute Warning: Time to Fight for What Matters Most* is for you. I want to encourage you to apply the thoughts and principles that Chris has written. Even though you may feel like your life is in the two-minute drill, take a deep breath and allow this book to help you along the way. I am excited to see how this book is going to add value to you as an athlete—but more importantly, as a child of God.

INTRODUCTION

The pages of this book cost me more than 30 years of my life. Days I cried. Days I celebrated. Some unforgettable days and some that I wish I could forget. There were even times over the years when God woke me up in the middle of the night. So, to say this book has been 30 years in the making is no exaggeration.

My name is Chris and I'm obsessed with impacting and influencing young people! Over the last 18 years, I've had the privilege of speaking to over 350,000 young people throughout the world in camps, counseling sessions, student clubs, church services, conferences, locker rooms, and more—yet, I haven't even made a dent in the big picture of reaching an entire generation. I once read that there are 40 *million* teens in the U.S. today. Just let that sink in for a second. The reality is, this is about more than one person. I'm just one part of the family of God. This is about raising and equipping leaders.

Thus, the writing of this book.

2-Minute Warning is a book for young people who are tired of just fitting in and following the crowd. It's for a generation who knows they aren't "normal," who know they were made for something greater. I'm sounding the alarm and challenging you to answer the call and take action now! At the end of specific chapters, there is a call-to-action segment called "2-Minute Drill." These aren't just suggestions; they're designed directives for you to stop and do something that will move you ahead in the game of life. Some will be more challenging than others, but hey, you're up for the challenge—or you wouldn't be reading this book, right?

. . . You're up for the challenge—or you wouldn't be reading this book!

If you're a student, athlete, or even someone who cares about this generation—a teacher, youth pastor, coach, lead pastor, counselor, parent, or maybe even a grandparent who has a heart for millennials and generation Z—then this book is for *you*!

This is an urgent call. Just as an emergency response team responds with urgency, you need to respond the same way. This book will challenge you to live your life like others depend on it because it's the truth.

There's a ton of material out there on how to get in physical shape and millions of diet and workout plans. There are leadership books, books on mental health, books on how to be a better coach, and books on how to build a business, but let me get this straight right from the beginning. This is about your SPIRIT and

SOUL. It's probably the part of you that gets the LEAST attention and work, yet it's the MOST IMPORTANT part of who you are. One day, we will all stand before God and all our trophies, bank accounts, number of social media followers and "Likes" will NOT matter. It's time to be 100% whole.

It's time to focus and fight for what matters most!

Are you ready?

Let's go!

1

FULL OF IT

One of the highlights of my middle school days was playing basketball. I loved everything about it and just knew I was bound for the NBA one day. Well, okay . . . not quite!

After one practice, I rode my bike to my aunt's house—tired, sweaty, and hungry. The moment I walked into her house, my mind was blown away by the amazing smells of spices and scents from a huge spread of Puerto Rican food. I said some really quick "Hello"s, dropped my bag, and headed straight for the kitchen. The food wasn't ready but that didn't stop me from going in for some quick samples. As soon as I stuck my hand out to reach for the food . . . SLAP! My aunt stood there and said, "Go get in the shower. You're sweaty, and you stink! Dinner will be ready in 20 minutes." "Twenty minutes?" I replied, "I'm hungry now!"

My desperate plea didn't change her mind.

Right then, I had three choices. One: to just listen and obey (which was too hard). Two: to try and overpower my aunt and grab some food (which would have had very bad consequences). Three: look for food elsewhere (the most logical answer for a 12-year-old hungry boy!). So, I headed to the garage cupboards (where all the snacks were stashed) and found my favorite—Ho-Ho's and Red Vines. Score! After eating four Ho-Ho's and two handfuls of Red Vines, my stomach was satisfied. The best part was that no one saw me. Now, I was ready to hit the showers.

After I had cleaned up and smelled better, it was time to eat. The table was set with a huge spread of food. We all sat down as a family, but there was one tiny problem: I was full! In traditional Latino families, adults serve their kids' plates. Kids don't serve themselves, because they tend to skip out on certain foods (**cough*, **cough*) . . . like vegetables! So, without any chance of fixing myself something small, my genius plan was at risk. My aunt served me first and put a full plate down right in front of me because, "I was so hungry." I stayed at that table the rest of the night, because I couldn't finish my plate. My aunt wasn't going to let me do anything else until it was all gone. My plan had seriously backfired, but I learned a lesson that night that has stayed with me my whole life.

God showed me how this whole scenario was actually a snapshot of today's generation who are filling themselves with so much "junk," that when it's time to eat the best food, they don't want it or even have a desire for it. They're just not hungry.

From the music played through their smartphones to every form of media, young people are fed a constant diet of sex, violence, porn, racial uprising, rebellion against authority, and drug abuse—all this while they load up their bodies on the worst possible foods on the planet (energy drinks and sodas with massive amounts of sugar, fast food, etc.).

G.I.G.O.

Back in the early '70s, there was a term in the computer world that said, "Garbage in, garbage out." Basically, it said that since computers can't think for themselves, whatever the user put in is what came out. Even though that was popular way before our time, it's still true today—not only regarding computers but in our everyday life, too.

A few years ago, I was hanging with some friends. One couple had a three-year-old boy. We were all hanging out in the living room when all of a sudden, this little boy blurts out, "Oh, sh—!" In the middle of all the adults laughing, the boy's parent jumped up and said, "Mijo, that's a bad word! Where did you hear that?" What's interesting is that we all know that this word was not automatically in this young kid's heart and mind. It was planted there. Somewhere along the line, this three-year-old heard someone use that word, and then naturally he repeated it.

Garbage in, garbage out.

YOU ARE WHAT YOU EAT

I hardly know any young person who hasn't heard the phrase, "You are what you eat,"—probably way more times than they wanted to. However, the reason you hear it so much is simple: because it's true. If you want to be physically healthy, you have to eat healthy food. Believe me, I eat more than my fair share of unhealthy fast food; but if that were the only thing I ate, I'd weigh 400 pounds! Thank God, my wife is a good cook.

Even when things change and shift, God's Word remains the same.

Now, let's bring this to a spiritual level. The number one way God communicates with us is through His Word—the Bible. Jesus described it as "our daily bread."[1] I once had a student tell me, "Chris, I go to church on Sundays and to my youth group on Wednesdays. Isn't that enough?" Of course, those are two important things to be actively a part of, but *nothing* replaces our time in God's Word. Remember, Jesus called it "daily," not "weekly" bread!

My pastor says it this way, "We must move from *corporate* encounters with God to *daily* encounters with Him." At no time in history was this more true than in 2020—the year a global pandemic threatened to close the doors of every church and youth group in America. What we learned was this: Even when things change and shift, God's Word remains the same.

Why is eating our daily bread important? Well, let's see what the Bible says about it:

"But He (Jesus) answered and said, 'It is written, "Man shall not live by bread alone, but by every word that proceeds from the mouth of God."'"[2]

"Your word is a lamp to my feet and a light to my path."[3]

"For the word of God is living and powerful, and sharper than any two-edged sword, piercing even to the division of soul and spirit, and of joints and marrow, and is a discerner of the thoughts and intents of the heart."[4]

"Heaven and earth shall pass away, but my words shall not pass away."[5]

Look at that diet! God's Word is the forever unchanging truth! He is our supply and guide throughout life. That's even better than my aunt's Puerto Rican spread! But, just reading the Word is only the beginning.

There is another step.

THE KEY

Here's what I want you to understand: The Bible was *never* meant to just be *read;* it's meant to be *lived*! Let's look it at through the eyes of sports.

The Bible wasn't meant to just be read; it's meant to be lived.

Just imagine you decided to get into the best shape of your life. You find one of the best professional strength and fitness coaches you can find and he agrees to train you. He gives you a full workout regimen and a daily nutrition plan—all proven to have been successful for his clients, which he has a full photo portfolio of before-and-afters to back it up! You even go out and buy a gym membership and all the food and food prep containers you need to prepare for your new fitness quest. You're ready to go!

Now, imagine going through all of that and making the huge financial investment . . . but NEVER putting it into action! What do you think would happen? You know exactly what would happen—NOTHING! You would never see those amazing results. That would be crazy, right?

Here's the key: You have to put that plan into *action*! Even if I memorized the workouts and knew the diet plan backwards and forwards, there would be *no transformation* until I put in the work.

The same is true in being a Christian—a Christ-follower. You can have knowledge of the God's Word, but you have to put it into action. James, who was the brother of Jesus, wrote it like this:

> *"But be doers of the word, and not hearers only, deceiving yourselves."*[6]

The power promised to you in the Bible only happens when you apply the Word AND do what it says. For example, when you choose to forgive, when you are kind to someone, when you are generous, and when you *obey* what God is saying and live by the truths in the Word, then you'll see a life change, a real transformation.

That dinner at my aunt's house was so good, I can close my

eyes and still smell it to this day! The table was spread. It's too bad I blew it by sneaking in some junk food before dinner. But how many of us do the same thing with the Word of God? The Bible is everywhere—on our computers, phones, laptops, social media platforms, and tons of apps to help us study it—you name it. The table is spread. All we have to do is come to the table hungry . . . and then eat.

We don't need man's opinion. Today, more than ever, we need the *truth* from the One who holds our lives in His hands—the One who proved to the world He was who He said He was when He rose from the grave. Fill your life with that! Don't pig out on spiritual junk food. Stay hungry for the real stuff. Remember, the Bible says when you stay hungry and thirsty after righteousness, you will be filled—with the good stuff.[7] What's the key?

Stay hungry . . . and obey!

2

THE STORM

For most of my life, I lived in California, and I have to tell you, it's nice—REALLY nice! There's hardly any other place on earth where you can surf in the ocean and snowboard down a mountain on the same day. The weather is perfect all year around . . . well, except for the occasional earthquake! Even so, I think it's the perfect place to live.

I remember sitting outside my house one day in beautiful 80-degree weather, reading about the tsunamis and hurricanes that had ravaged through cities around the world. The damage was tremendous. From people losing their homes to some who had lost their lives, all of it was heartbreaking. This was something we had never experienced in California and I was overwhelmed by what I saw and read.

Isn't it amazing that today's technology not only allows us the ability to read about storms that happen all over the world, but it also gives us the ability to detect storms that are on the way to a specific location? This information gives people time to prepare and evacuate if necessary.

The same is true about spiritual storms—but with warnings much more accurate than technology: the Holy Spirit.

Not long after this, God showed me a huge storm that is ravaging the lives of young people. It gives very little warning and is already here with full force. This storm is an equal opportunity destroyer—not taking into consideration skin color, how much money you have or don't, or what faith you belong to. It has only one goal for this generation: to do as much damage as possible. Like all major storms, it even has a name.

"Perversion."

UNDER THE INFLUENCE

Young person, you are being attacked in *every* area imaginable. The storm of perversion is bombarding young people, just like you, every day through every media source out there—the Internet, TV, mobile apps, movies, and music. It comes quickly and doesn't ask for permission Of course, it's downplayed as "no big deal," but the truth is that perversion is today's biggest public message with untold hidden consequences.

When I was in elementary school, it seemed like everyone had heroes that we all looked up to—people we wanted to be like because their lives had such an impact in the world, in our community, and in others. Today, we don't have heroes anymore; we have *celebrities.* There's something wrong with our world when America's biggest celebrities are famous for their scandals, perversion, raunchy videos, and warped lyrics. Real heroes aren't the latest social media sensations or reality show stars; real heroes are those who give their lives for causes that are bigger than they are. Real heroes are people like those serving in our military, coaches who do way more than just coach, single parents who sacrifice their dreams and goals for their kids, teachers who invest in our youth, and more. These are the people worth following and pursuing—the ones whose voices should be sought out, heard, and valued.

Of course, the greatest hero of all time is Jesus Christ.

I want you to stop and think about what TV, music, and media was like for your parents and grandparents. What were some of the shows they watched or music they heard? I can guarantee you it wasn't like Katy Perry's 2010 number one radio hit, "California Gurls," which has sold over five million tracks and counting! The song says this:

"California girls, we're unforgettable
Daisy Dukes, bikinis on top
Sun-kissed skin, so hot, we'll melt your popsicle . . .

Sex on the beach
We don't mind sand in our stilettos
We freak in my Jeep
Snoop Doggy Dog on the stereo!"[1]

Melting popsicles, sex on the beach, and freaking in Jeeps should be shocking to you. But it isn't! Instead, it's cool, edgy, and "in." No big deal right? Ok, how about 2020 number one hit "WAP" by Cardi B. Really? 300 MILLION streams on YouTube and Spotify. Why? Because our culture has targeted *you,* and it started the day you were born. Want proof? Do you know that "California Gurls" song is featured on one of the multi-million-selling video game series called *Just Dance* and is also on the popular kids' music CD, *Kidz Bop*? What?! So, today, we have eight and 10-year-olds walking through their houses singing and dancing to this song . . . in front of their parents . . . and with no recourse whatsoever. Sadly, the parents are the ones who probably bought it for them.

Welcome to the storm called "perversion."

Here's what the creator of MTV and iHeart Media, Bob Pittman, thinks about influencing you:

> *"The strongest appeal you can make is emotional. If you can get their (youth) emotions going, make them forget their logic, you've got them. At MTV, we don't shoot for the 14-year-olds, we OWN them."*[2]

When perversion comes in, rebellion comes out.

Pittman and Hollywood have been greatly successful at their goal. They have helped shape a generation into violent, unaccountable, purposeless pleasure-seekers who instead of thinking for themselves, simply mirror what they've been told to believe. This has resulted in addictive and destructive behaviors, which is nothing more than straight-up rebellion.

Over the years, I've seen so many students who couldn't sit still or pay attention in church or school for 50 minutes sit and watch a two-and-a-half-hour horror movie without moving. Youth today are under the influence.

There is an attack on you and most of your parents are clueless.

The equation is simple: When perversion comes in, rebellion comes out. How can you tell if you're being overtaken by this storm? It's like this: Your parents ask you to do a chore and this anger and attitude come out. Or, a friend is pushing you to do something shady and instead of being bothered by it, it excites you. When you find yourself throwing all common sense out the window and jumping into these things . . . welcome to rebellion!

What's even crazier about this storm of perversion is that it is so strong that most young people don't even think things like porn and getting physical before marriage are "harmful" or "bad" anymore. They've pretty much become the norm. It's become normal to see a fight breakout at school or in the neighborhood and no one try to break it up. Instead, onlookers are quick to pull out their phones, so they can start recording it, cheer it on, and then post it to their social media profiles.

Things are getting worse and worse, yet our culture is doing nothing to stop it. They're just like the people who pull out their cell phones to video it—except they're doing it on a much bigger scale by making reality shows about it and then making millions off of it by marketing it to you.

Something's gotta change!

I thank God that He is raising a generation that isn't comfortable with the "norm!" He's raising an army that isn't happy with, nor will settle for the "norm!"

He's raising Culture Changers. (We'll talk more about that in the next chapter.)

VOICES, VOICES

Could it be that if someone hears the same message over and over again, that they begin to believe it and then live it? That's exactly what's happening under our watch. There is an attack on you and most of your parents are clueless. The celebs blame your parents for this behavior, while most parents blame the culture. In the end, *you* are the ones dying and paying for it.

I can't count how many parents have come to me over the years and have said, "We never raised our kid to talk that way. Why are they cussing?" Or they ask things like, "How could she get pregnant?" or "What happened to their grades?" My answer, in love, has always been, "Maybe *you* didn't raise them as much as you think. Maybe they look and sound exactly like the ones who did raise them—the culture!"

What if the loudest voice in my life is actually not the best voice for me to be listening to?

There are a host of voices trying to get your attention. Oftentimes, you don't even realize the voices you're listening to. Until you stop and examine this, you will continue to just follow any voice coming your way. Sometimes, you just follow the loudest one. Thanks to social media, TV, the Internet, magazines, billboards, and dozens of other places, you're able to compare yourself to thousands of different images each week. For some, it's a thousand a day!

The average young person is on their phone eight hours a day. For some, the loudest voice is video games or friends or music and their favorite artists. What or who is the biggest, the loudest voice in your life right now? More importantly, ask yourself this: What if the loudest voice in my life is actually not the best voice for me to be listening to?

My guess is if you're reading this, you're not satisfied with the other voices and you want God's voice to be the loudest. Any other voice will leave you broken, misled, and unsatisfied.

THE TWO-PART YOU

In this battle for *your* generation, the stakes are high. Why? Because they know that the winner will have control and influence over you for the next 50 to 100 years. The Bible puts it this way:

> *"For our struggle is not against flesh and blood, but against the rulers, against the authorities, against the powers of this dark world and against the spiritual forces of evil in the heavenly realms."*[3]

This war is a spiritual one! Spiritual? Yes! You were created in the physical but with a spirit. I remember a big-time football coach once asked me, "How are you going to help me win football games?" I said, "Coach, I believe God created us with two dynamics—a physical side and a spiritual side. Right now, you're coaching the outside, but you have no one coaching the inside—the heart and spirit. You have 53 half-hearted players because you don't address the inside! I will do that. I will help you get 100% out of these players and coaches."

Living your life and only investing in your physical side is like living in a two-story house and never going upstairs! It's there, but you never get to enjoy it. To weather this storm and win this war, you *must* invest in your spiritual side. When you pass from this earth, your physical side will die but your spiritual side will live forever. So, you must look at your spiritual side as being even *more* important than your physical side!

What are you doing right now to invest in your spiritual side? You cannot be a part-time soldier in this full-time war against you and for your generation. It's time to step up your game and go all-in!

The storm is here and the battle is raging. As you read this book, my prayer is that the fire in your spirit burns hotter and hotter. I pray as you move forward that this book gives you more than just an emotional high, but *real tools* to not just settle for playing the defense. It's time to get on the offense!

Let's go!

3

CULTURE CHANGERS

One of the hottest topics in the news right now is about the whole "cancel culture." It's a heavily debated and highly controversial topic out there right now and people on every side have very opinionated views either way. FYI: This chapter is NOT about canceling culture but about changing it!

With all the things that are destroying this generation, like I said before, I believe God is raising an army of "Culture Changers." A Culture Changer is simply a devout and passionate follower of Jesus sent into the world to make an impact. They're not afraid of the darkness, because they have the power of the Light. They're not intimidated by opposition, because the One in them is greater. Culture Changers don't just settle for good or even great results; they desire God-ideas and God-results. They're tired of the current religious model and playing church. They want a real move of God. These are a remnant of Believers who are passionate about being the hands and feet of Jesus to the world. With Culture Changers, His presence has become their priority and their pursuit.

I specifically used the word "army," a military term, to describe the type of Culture Changers God is raising up for this time in history. When you join the military, they don't send you directly to a war zone. Knowing nothing about combat, military procedures, and military strategies, you would be of no use to them there and would probably end up getting yourself and other fellow soldiers killed. So, when you enlist, the first thing they do is send you to boot camp where you get the best training possible. They help BUILD you into a soldier and EQUIP you for war.

With Culture Changers, His presence has become their priority and their pursuit.

In the same way, a Culture Changer is one who is equipped and ready to fight. No, not a physical fight, but the fight we all face in life as we go through daily struggles and deal with difficult issues.

Throughout the years, I have come to the conclusion that every young person who wants to be a Culture Changer must win five battles they *all* will face, which we will deal with individually here in this book. With God's Holy Spirit and a strong support team (family, pastors, mentors, friends, etc.), you will win these battles and impact your culture for God's purpose. Not only do I believe in you, but God does, too.

Think about this for a second. Out of all the time periods you could have been born in, God designed you to live in the *here* and *now,* which means He believes you can impact this planet for His glory. Would you take a second, put down this book, and just meditate on that for a few minutes? You get one shot at this thing called life! In this life, we are in the two-minute warning and the time clock is ticking. Every moment matters. God's design for you is to live life like His son, Jesus, and live it in a *legendary* way—legendary, in that your life was designed to impact generations!

Out of all the time periods you could have been born in, God designed you to live in the here and now, . . .

The reality is your life will impact those coming behind you. The question is, "What kind of impact will you have?" One that will be great or one that you will regret? Your life was designed to impact eternity.

Now, here's a crazy thought: There's only one thing you can take to Heaven. One thing! That one thing—other people.

WHO DO YOU REP?

When someone mentions the craziest fans, chances are one particular team instantly comes to mind. Maybe it's even your team. The Raiders almost always makes the top of that list! Their fans are insanely fanatical—and we actually think it's cool and normal and love to watch them!

It's great to have a favorite sports team. As a matter of fact, it gives us a cause to support and a connection to other fans. Most sports fans proudly display their support, spending huge amounts of money on team merchandise. Many even go to the expense of traveling to away games just to show their support for their team.

Some extreme fans paint their faces and wear crazy costumes to display their support for their team, such as two crazy pro hockey fans who recently became pretty popular for the extreme measures they take to support their Vancouver team. At every major team game, these two fanatics dress in head-to-toe green outfits and buy tickets for the seats closest to the penalty box just for the purpose of distracting the opposing team's players! It's pretty funny. These guys, they go all out and are all in!

Maybe you haven't thought about it before but being a follower of Jesus is similar to being a sports fan. We have a awesome cause to support, and we should want to support that proudly and boldly in every area of our life! We, too should go all out and be all in! Afterall, His record is perfect, and He always wins. Never a losing season. He's the champion who is worth it all and gave His all!

I was thinking about being a "fan" for Christ and came across these verses in the Bible:

"And he died for all, that those who live should no longer live for themselves but for him who died for them and was raised again. So from now on we regard no one from a worldly point of view. Though we once regarded Christ in this way, we do so no longer. Therefore, if anyone is in Christ, the new creation has come: The old has gone, the new is here! All this is

> *from God, who reconciled us to himself through Christ and gave us the ministry of reconciliation: that God was reconciling the world to himself in Christ, not counting people's sins against them. And he has committed to us the message of reconciliation. We are therefore Christ's ambassadors, as though God were making his appeal through us."*[1]

Think about these verses in relation to what Christ did for us and how, when we recognize the truth in them, we should want to tell everyone we know about Him. We are literally Christ's ambassadors or "representatives" here on this planet! What a privilege and an honor that God chose us—you and I—to do that job! That means He believes we can do it with His help. Our job is to tell other people about Jesus and give them the opportunity to experience reconciliation. Reconciliation is when we receive God's forgiveness for our sins and begin a lifelong relationship with Jesus.

So, the question is: How do we represent Jesus to this world?

Personally, I love Christian t-shirts, hats, and jewelry and have a lot of them. But does that make me a representative of Christ? No, not necessarily. I even attend church on a weekly basis—sometimes, several times a week. Does that make me a representative? No, not necessarily.

Don't get me wrong; those things are important, but I believe there are two HUGE things that matter most to Jesus: our ATTITUDES and our ACTIONS.

You and I have the chance to be positive, solid representatives of Jesus through our actions and attitudes. This doesn't mean we have to be perfect, but it does mean we have to be authentic. It means that we love people, we display compassion, we meet the needs of people, we forgive, we clothe the naked and feed the hungry, and we show kindness to others. When we do these Christ-like things and have a Christ-like attitude, we are revealing Jesus to our world.

It's interesting because Jesus never called His followers "Christians." The word "Christian" was given to people from non-believers who acted and followed the teachings of Christ. They didn't know how to describe these people who were so different than everyone else. All they could say was, "They're Christians!" (Followers of Christ!)

You and I have the chance to be positive, solid representatives of Jesus through our actions and attitudes.

Following Jesus starts on the inside and works its way to the outside. Sadly, this world says the opposite: "Hey, if you have money, power, a great job, and fame, THEN you will have joy, peace, and happiness!"

So, let me ask you something?

Who do *you* represent? Who would your friends and co-workers say you represent? You see, if Christ's teachings don't motivate you to take action, then it's nothing but empty words and religious talk. It's just theory—and theory doesn't change lives! It never has, and it never will.

If you're a student, you're probably thinking right about now, *Hang on, Chris! I'm still in school! This stuff is for much later in life.* Oh, but is it? Let me tell you that your school years are really important, and they *will* affect the rest of your life. Believe me, they matter. These years play a pivotal role in shaping who you are and who you are going to be. These are the years when you are deciding who you are, where you fit in, and what role you play in the bigger story of the world. When you were back in elementary school, you didn't have to answer these questions; because they were answered for you by your parents, teachers, and just about anyone around you.

That was then, this is now.

So, are you ready to join a movement that will make an impact on people both now and for eternity? Are you ready to give yourself to a cause and mission that was instituted by Jesus Himself? Ready to be a world-changer? A Culture Changer? If so, then let's do this. Time is running out. We are definitely at the two-minute warning. Time to keep fighting.

The next chapter will help you do just that, as we look at the five battles I believe every Culture Changer faces—and must win.

4

THE BATTLE FOR IDENTITY

Mark Twain once said, "The two most important days in your life are the day you were born and the day you find out why." I like to say it like this: "It's the day you discover *whose* you are and the day you discover *who* you are." Are you just an accident? A result of life's coincidences? Or is there a purpose—something strategic for something greater? In searching for answers, you'll find that your true identity is tied to the Creator of everything—God. You'll never know who you are until you know who *He* is.

One day when I came home from working with some coaches and athletes, my daughter Mayah (who was three years old at the time) brought me a drawing that she had created just for me. I loved it! Why? Because *she made* it . . . and I love *her*. She created something for me out of the love in her heart. That love caused her to stop watching *Paw Patrol* (or whatever show she was watching), get up, go get the materials, and make my surprise. I was blown away.

After she handed it to me, she asked two questions. *"Daddy, do you like it?"* in which I told her, *"I love it because you made this just for me."* Then she asked a question that caught me by surprise: *"Daddy, do you know what it is?"* The truth is, it was scribbled Crayon all over a piece of paper and I had no clue what it was! I quickly looked at my wife for help. She tried to give it her best interpretation but was incorrect. The last thing I wanted to do was to guess and not get it right. So, I responded, *"Mayah, I love this because you made it. What is it?"* To which she replied, "Elmo!" Even though her drawing looked nothing like Elmo, this three-year-old taught me a huge lesson that day:

If you're trying to discover the purpose and meaning of a design, you have to go straight to the creator. In the same way, if you are having trouble finding your purpose in life or understanding what you were put on this earth to do, especially when nothing in your life so far makes any sense to you, you have to go to the One who created you—God—and allow Him to reveal that to you. The day you find that out will change your life forever!

GET TO THE ROOT

Let me make this clear. The most valuable thing about you is that God, Himself, created you. Period. It's not your gifts and talents, where you were born, or how much money you have in the bank. If your identity is found in something you *do* or what you *have*, then it's based in the wrong place.

So many people today are chasing social media followers and "Likes," but in reality, what they really want is love—real, authentic, unconditional, selfless love. The problem is, no person can give that type of love to the degree they seek. That love can only be found in Jesus Christ. Think about my daughter's story. What an amazing example of God's love for your life. God created every single person on this planet out of the love in His heart. Just like my daughter was moved by love to take action, so did God.

Let me explain it this way. Let's say I bought a football from a store for $75. If I played a game with it and signed it, guess how much it would be worth? That's right, 75 bucks! The value wouldn't change because of who I am. Now, let Tom Brady use it for a game and then sign it. That $75 football now becomes $2,000 or more simply because of whose hands were on it! We're just talking about a person, but look what the Bible says about God:

> *"So God created man in His own image; in the image of God He created him; male and female he created them."*[1]

God is the only one with the authority to declare who you are and why you matter. You were made with a reflection of Him in you. Just stop for a second and say this: *"God, the creator of the universe, of every star in the sky and of every planet, created me!"*

God is the only one with the authority to declare who you are and why you matter.

This is so important to understand because it's the first message you receive from God concerning your identity. The problem is, sin messed it up! (We will see how in our next chapter.) But that doesn't mean the image of God in you was lost. No, it's only that God's authoritative message about *who you are* no longer satisfies you like it used to. This causes an identity crisis . . . and sin is the root issue!

But we're about to conquer that.

THE KEY: WHAT YOU BELIEVE

Today's generation is in an identity crisis like never before. Young people today don't know if they're straight, gay, bi, trans, or even the same gender that God made them! It's craziness to the 100th power. Sadly, most people don't even know what the word "identity" even means. Identity can be best explained as *the condition or character as to who a person is* and there's no better place to find it than the Bible! Let's look at two areas to help explain this even more.

#1

YOU WERE MADE BY GOD AND FOR GOD

Think about this question: Is your identity determined by what you do or is what you do determined by your identity? According to the Bible, God wants you to know *who* you are, first, so you can start living accordingly. Being a child of God—someone who is alive and free in Christ—should determine what you do and how you see life.

What you believe will always show up in your actions. For example, if I wanted to know what you believe about your grades, all I have to do is see your report card. It's the same way spiritually. What do you believe about God? Do you just believe *in* God, or do you believe in *who He is*? The Bible says even demons believe in God! But, who do *you* say He is? This is the greatest question we all have to answer with our lives. Is He a lunatic, a liar, or is He really LORD? We find this question in the Bible, when Jesus asked His disciples this:

What you believe will always show up in your actions.

> *"When Jesus came in the region of Caesarea Philippi, he asked his disciples, 'Who do people say the Son of Man is?' They replied, 'Some say John the Baptist; others say Elijah; and still others, Jeremiah or one of the prophets.' But what about you? he asked. Who do you say I am? Simon Peter answered, 'You are the Messiah, the Son of the living God.'"*[2]

Again, your actions say what you believe. If you love the Golden State Warriors, like I do, it will cause you to buy a jersey and maybe even a hat. You will post about them and follow them on social media, and take time to go to games or watch them on TV. It becomes evident what team you love. Let's take that a step further. Like Peter (in the Bible), you might believe that Jesus is the Son of God, but do your friends believe you believe?

How about your family? Teammates? If I asked them what you believe, what would they say? It's one thing to believe, but a whole other step for those around you to know it because it's seen through your life.

The Bible makes it clear that you are God's masterpiece, created in Christ Jesus, so you can accomplish all the good things He has planned for you. Another translation of that scripture says that you are God's handiwork. King David said it like this:

> *"For you created my inmost being; you knit me together in my mother's womb. I praise you because I am fearfully and wonderfully made; your works are wonderful, I know that full well. My frame was not hidden from you when I was made in the secret place. When I was woven together in the depths of the earth, your eyes saw my unformed body."*[3]

Notice the word "made." David didn't use this word like you would "make" a sandwich or you "made" a good pass. No, this specific word, "raqam," is only found one other time in the Bible—when describing where the Israelites worshipped before the temple was built. This word refers to the skill or the handiwork of God to create His masterpiece with expertise and precision. Not just anyone could pull off this job. This took extraordinary skill and love to make it. When David uses the word "made," he speaks of the weaver, the Creator Himself, and His attention to detail and intentionality with which He created us.

In short, King David was simply saying, "It is from God, and through God, and because of God that I have worth." Regardless of how many voices the king heard, His identity rested in one reason and one reason alone—because God made him!

If you have never been told you are valuable or that you matter, I get the privilege right now to tell you. YOU MATTER! YOU ARE VALUABLE!

Whether you know it or not, God has placed in every single person a unique set of gifts and abilities to fix something. When you seek God, you can put all these things together to discover your calling, passion, and mission.

My friend, Samuel, is a great example. He had a huge passion to see people come out of poverty, especially in his home country of Romania where he grew up in poverty. After seeking God about this, he used his creativity to design cool rain boots and then started a company called Roma Boots. From the beginning, the company has donated a pair of boots to someone who is underprivileged for every pair sold. Roma Boots exploded, which allowed Samuel to travel the world and have a global impact. He's even been featured on major TV shows like *Good Morning America.* To date, Roma Boots has donated tens of thousands of boots in 25 countries across five continents!

One of the most remarkable and inspiring things in life is to watch people learn their purpose and then walk in it—people like Samuel, a legit Culture Changer and real hero. He's not alone. You, too are destined for greatness!

Before you can see who you *are*, it's important to know who you *were*. The Bible is very clear on the subject. Every person on the planet was born with two conditions: *in sin* and *without God.* In our culture, it's very popular for people to say, "I was born this way," which they are right! Everyone is born into sin.

In the very beginning when God created the earth and everything in it, we see where He created Adam and Eve, the first people. (See Genesis Chapter 2.) They were perfect and enjoyed being in the presence of God all the time. But then, one day, they were tempted and made a horrible choice to believe a lie. From that moment the curse of sin was birthed and immediately their identity was broken. They realized that they were naked and were so ashamed that they even tried to hide from God.

But here's the awesome thing: God sent Jesus to die on a cross for us, so we could be re-connected to our identity in Christ. All we have to do is become born "again," which is what happens when we ask Christ to come into our heart and make the decision to live for Him. As a matter of fact, to fulfill the specific assignment God has for you will require this second birth.

The biggest and most important battle for Culture Changers is over the question Jesus asked His 12 disciples: "Who do you say I am?" He's still asking that same thing today. Do you live under God's identity or your own? Understanding this is of utmost importance because, again, *your actions always follow what you believe!*

Notice that Jesus didn't ask what Peter's friend, parents, or even his youth pastor thought about Him. Jesus wanted to hear what *Peter* thought! Right now, He's asking you the same thing: "Who do YOU say I am?" Think about this. Who is Jesus to you? Is He a friend? A religion? Was He just a teacher? A good man? A good storyteller? Or is He your Lord? The bottom line: Who is He to *you*?

If you don't trust God's Word for your truth, then where does it come from? One word: culture—and take a look at what is being sold to us about our identity.

These are only partial lyrics to a few songs that sold millions:

- *"And Jesus can't save you. Life starts when the church ends."* - Jay Z, "Empire State of Mind"
- *"Players only, come on . . . second verse for the hustlas, gangstas, bad b*tches and ya ugly a** friends. Can I preach? I gotta show em how a PIMP get in . . ."* – Bruno Mars, "24 Carat Gold"
- *"I kissed a girl, and I liked it."* – Katy Perry

These stars have the biggest followings on social media impacting millions every day with each tweet, each song, and each video they post preaching a message loud and clear.

Most-viewed TV shows with the highest ratings are: *13 Reasons Why*, *Euphoria*, *Bridgerton*, *Keeping Up with the Kardashians*, and *Riverdale.* All these celebrate bad language and sexual situations. By exposing our young people to these attitudes and behavior, their goal is to make us think and feel like it's normal. It's the way we should live. And every single day, they are targeting YOU!

I can go on and on, but you get the picture, if you're honest with yourself. In high school, as I watched and listened to culture's top stars, I couldn't help but to want to talk like them, party like them, and be like them. It definitely didn't push me to be my best or to be more like Christ.

Don't let a godless world tell you who God is and who you are!

The bottom line is this: Don't let a godless world tell you who God is and who you are! The Bible should be your mirror—the ONLY place you look to see who you really are. The Word of God is where you discover *whose* you are and *who* you are!

Do you realize that you were born a blank canvas? But, soon, people began to paint a picture that started to shape your identity. Most of those strokes were painted by words spoken over you, about you, or directly to you. Never forget that *words are* powerful! Be careful who you allow to speak into your life.

Life experiences—whether good or bad—paint on your canvas and shape your identity, as well. Just because something bad happened to you does not mean you're a bad person or that your future is bad. Let the Bible, not your experiences, be the lenses through which you view life. Experiences can *refine* you, but they do not have to *define* you!

That's God's job.

Every school has its fair share of cliques: jocks, nerds, goths, cowboys, gamers, the plastics (Watch *Mean Girls* for the definition!), and even gangs. It's sad to watch so many young people grab their identity from a group that they will probably never see again after graduation. You were born an original, don't die a copy. Let me tell you, your identity is so much deeper! It goes beyond cliques, background, and skin color. Don't get me wrong. Experiences are important. Culture is important. Family and the people who influence you are important. But none of these come close to the input that comes from your Creator—God!

Experiences can refine you, but they do not have to define you!

What God has to say about you is more important than anybody else's opinion. There is *no one* more passionate about you than God! His passion and extreme love for you caused Him to send His Son, Jesus, to pay the ultimate price for your freedom!

Now, let's check out number two!

#2

YOUR IDENTITY IS RESTORED THROUGH CHRIST AND FOUND IN CHRIST

Let me reinforce something here: Your value doesn't come from what you look like, the things you have, or what you do. Your worth comes from the One who did the work of creating, designing, and making you unique! So, what does that mean for you? Very simply, it means you have value. You have worth. You have purpose and meaning. How do I know that? Because the God of the universe created you! Why would everything He made on the planet have purpose and not you? The chair you're sitting in, TV's, phones, desks, helmets—all were created with purpose. One of the saddest things on the planet is for someone to exist, to not know they have purpose and to not know what that purpose is. What's even more sad? It's for someone to just "exist," to know they have purpose yet never function in that purpose.

My kids, for example, are the best at using things in ways they were not intended for them to be used. My Costco empty boxes become boats, chairs and blankets turn into a fort, and sticks become swords. They may have given my kids hours of fun, but they were definitely not made for that purpose. See what I mean? It is possible for you to exist and never walk in your true identity and purpose.

Listen, God knows you better than you know yourself! It's true, and it's good news. When you understand this truth, it will change the way you live and think. It means you can stop hating what you see in the mirror or what you hear from others. It means you stop looking to culture and your so-called friends to communicate a message that no one but God has the right to communicate. Friends will fade; movements will die out; culture will change, but God's Word stays the same forever!

Everyone was created by God, which makes all seven billion people on the planet creations of God. But God's desire is for you to move from being a *creation* to being His *child*. There's a huge difference. Moving from His creation to His child only comes through surrendering your life to Him and allowing Him to adopt you into His family. And guess what? When you are a child of God, you have access to God that you didn't have before.

It's the privilege of relationship!

I've had the awesome opportunity of working with professional athletes for over a decade. It's been a great experience for me, but even more so for my kids. They have enjoyed some really cool experiences simply because of their relationship with me. From free tickets to games all the way to being brought onto playing fields at sporting events—they've experienced a lot of things that others haven't . . . all because of the privilege of relationship.

Words can shape you into something that you were never created to be. With that in mind, I want to give you a declaration and prayer that a pastor taught me. It goes like this:

"I am who God says I am—a child of God and the righteousness of God. I am the apple of God's eye. I am God's workmanship, created for good works and I can do all things through Christ who strengthens me. Today, I open up my mind to receive the Word of God, so that I can think like God, be like God, and do life the way God intended for me to live. Come, Holy Spirit, and help me elevate my thinking, so I can elevate my life. In Jesus' name. Amen!"

This is good for every believer in Jesus to declare. So, I challenge you to read this out loud every morning when you wake up. You might not even believe it at first, but keep doing it—every morning. Soon, what you hear will change what you believe. And what happens next?

You'll start to act like you believe!

2-MINUTE DRILL

If there was one word to describe who you think and feel you are, what would it be? If you had a name tag that everyone saw, what would it say? "Hello, my name is Hurt," ". . . Lonely," ". . . Broken," ". . . Lost," ". . . Fake." Would it be "Unworthy," "Follower," or "Loser"?

Ask God right now to speak a NEW word over your life according to His truth and ask that He would expose any lie you have believed over yourself. I believe someone reading these words will hear the words "Healed," "Worthy," "Champion," "Victorious," "Loved," "Forgiven," and more!

ROBERT GUERRERO

4-TIME BOXING WORLD CHAMPION

One day, I was on the sidelines before an Oakland Raider game. Celebs always came to the games, so it was normal to see M.C. Hammer, Ice Cube, Carlos Santana, Tiger Woods, Arnold Schwarzenegger, and more. I never bothered any of them, but on this particular Sunday, I saw boxing world champion Robert Guerrero. What stood out to me about this rising star wasn't his physique, but the shorts he wore in the ring during a fight. They had Acts 2:38 on them. I also noticed that every time he was interviewed, he talked about God. He was different.

I had the privilege of spending some time with Robert that day, and later I asked him his thoughts on the battle of faith and identity. His remarks were golden.

"Identity is everything. It shapes who we are and what we become. It's how people see me and see us. Or more importantly, can they see Christ is us?

For me in my journey, God brought a man into my life who would become my manager in the boxing world, Bob Santos. He came to recruit my brother, Victor, one day in our gym but noticed me hitting the heavy bag. Bob asked my Dad about me because I was a lefty and had good footwork. I was impressed by how he conducted himself and how he did business, so I asked him to be my manager. He only wanted to help me, but I felt we were supposed to work together.

Bob and I became very close and developed a strong relationship. He always put God first in everything he did. We started and ended our days with prayer. He was always upfront with me and very honest. I started asking questions about life and why he loved God. Up until then, my identity was in my sport—in being a boxer. So, when things didn't go well in the ring, it affected me greatly outside of the ring. If for some reason boxing would've been taken from me, my world would've crumbled.

My deep passion and dream was to be a champion but something inside was missing. In February of 2005, I was convinced Jesus Christ was who He said He was, and I gave my life to Him. I then got baptized. My identity changed. Boxing was no longer who I was; it was now something that I did and a tool that God would use in my life for His glory. My new identity was that of a child of God who was loved.

For the rest of my career, I would wear the Bible verse Acts 2:38 on my boxing trunks. I started to thank God with every win, and even in my tough losses. Most of the boxing community wasn't excited about this change in my life. No one really wanted to hear it, but I wanted every fan and every spectator to know I wasn't like everyone else! Maybe there's someone in the audience who would never step foot in a church, but they heard me or saw something in my life that pointed them to Jesus! Then it would all be worth it.

My biggest fight was in 2007 when I defended my IBF World Champion title against Martin Honorio. One week before the fight, on November 3, we got the news that my wife Casey was diagnosed with Leukemia, a life-threatening blood cancer. We had dated since junior high school. She was my lifelong sweetheart. Now, my world was shaken. What do I do? We had two young children and my career was really taking off . . . and then this hit! The thought of losing my wife was overwhelming. I turned to God, got on my knees, and cried out.

I decided that my wife was more important than my boxing career and that I needed to pull out of the upcoming fight. But something in my wife wouldn't let me. She told me that I needed to do it. So, I flew out the night before the fight was scheduled. When it was time for the bout, I was graced with a knockout victory just 56 seconds into the first round! It was one of the fastest knockouts in featherweight history.

She was right.

The next three years of my career would be some of the toughest moments. There were highs of her going into remission and lows of the cancer coming back. Many days of being by my wife's side, sleeping in that hospital room, and taking care of the kids. In January 2010, my wife got her bone marrow transplant. That, in itself, was a miracle as most people never find a match.

Her recovery was rough. After much prayer and seeking God, I decided to give up my championship belts and be by my wife's side full-time. That meant turning away huge paydays and opportunities to advance my career, but I had peace and knew God wanted me home. I also knew that she would be healed.

People thought I was crazy, but sometimes the hardest things and the right things are the same things! After many hard and tough months, my wife defeated her opponent called Leukemia and returned home. For me, that meant starting back on the bottom of the boxing world and working my way up to the top.

One of those memorable moments was an opportunity to fight Floyd "Money" Mayweather on Pay-Per-View for all the belts. The stage was set. Everything I had dreamed of was here.

MGM Grand, May 4, 2013. I walked into the ring wearing our team shirts that said, "God is GREAT." I felt great, had a good camp, and was confident this was going to be my night. In front of millions, I won the first three rounds. This was huge because Floyd had rarely lost a round in his entire career. But as I gave my everything in the ring against one of the greatest, I came up short and lost in a unanimous decision.

That was a tough pill to swallow. Many questions ran through my head. As I walked back into my locker room—with all the cameras following me and my family still proud of me—it hit me. There in that locker room was Chris Avilla waiting for me. He always prayed with me and our team after every fight. That night, I pointed at him and said, "We DID IT. We gave it our best and gave God the glory! We did it." After we prayed, I left confident that even though we didn't get what we wanted, I still knew who I was—a warrior for God.

Today, I'm still on that journey, and God uses it all for His glory."

@ghostboxing

5

THE BATTLE FOR PURITY

This battle has been giving out "L's" for years and it seems that boundaries are pushed more and more and younger and younger. The average age of kids experiencing porn is 11. People are starting out in marriages with destructive habits and false ideas that have caused the divorce rate to skyrocket. This is the battle for purity. So. let's start this chapter by understanding what purity really is. Purity is *a result of living for Jesus daily*. It's not something you earn; purity is a gift from Jesus.

Honestly, it's when you have an encounter with God and a REAL heart transformation that the Holy Spirit (God's Spirit) begins to empower you to start pursuing the right things. As someone pursuing God and His best for your life, you need to make it a priority to live pure. When you understand that you're not on this planet to just take up space, but that you have a calling and a purpose, then purity is a natural flow from your life. You might be asking, "How in the world can I stay pure in today's world?" This question isn't new and brings us to one of my favorite characters in the Bible. King David asked the same thing way back in the Old Testament:

> *"How can a young person stay pure? By obeying your word. I have tried hard to find you—don't let me wander from your commands. I have hidden your word in my heart, that I might not sin against you."*[1]

Notice, He not only asked the question but also gave the answer! How do you stay pure? By living according to the Word of God! That was back then. Today, we know that Jesus is the Word. So, how do you live in purity? By having Jesus in your heart and His Word on your mind. Let's face it, you're going to live by someone's design, so it might as well be God's! Purity is God's best model for your life.

RULES OF THE ROAD

I was so excited to get my driver's license when I turned 16. I studied that book so much that I aced my test! If you have your license or are in the process of getting it, one thing you will see about the handbook is how it's designed for one thing: to keep you safe. Stop signs, one-way signs, caution signs, speed limit signs—all of them are placed on the road so you don't hurt yourself or someone else. Those road signs aren't there to take the fun out of driving. No, they are there so you can *keep* driving and not wind up injured. This is exactly how God designed purity.

When it comes to living a life of purity, God has given you

the handbook. It's called the Bible! In it, God created some rules for the road—not to take away your fun but to keep you safe. It's funny because you never hear a police officer or parent say, "Our state has so many driving rules because we're trying to take away all the fun!" That would be crazy. But for some reason, people think that of God! They see Him as some giant killjoy just trying to make your young life miserable.

That couldn't be further from the truth.

As a matter of fact, God created sex! If anyone understands and knows how it works best, it would be the One who created it, right? God says throughout His Word that the *best* way is between one man and one woman in the boundaries of a holy marriage—a commitment to Him and to each other for life. Anything outside of that is dangerous and will hurt you and others. The problem is this: Your enemy (the devil) wants to tempt you with the *right thing*, the *wrong way*. His job is to always pervert what God has created.

It's called sin.

Sin is never satisfied. . . . It constantly wants more.

NEVER ENOUGH

There's a principle that most young people do not understand. Here it is: Sin never stays stagnant! Sin is never satisfied. It constantly wants more.

I had my first girlfriend in the sixth grade. I was so into sports at that time that I wasn't looking for anyone. But this girl in my homeroom class began pursuing me by writing letters and talking to me. My friends started to mount pressure on me to date her. (At 12-years-old, I really didn't even know what that meant!) So, I decided to jump into this relationship and become her boyfriend. For me, this meant walking around school holding hands. I remember my first attempt. My adrenaline was rushing as every scenario raced through my head. Then, I finally got the boldness to hold her hand. I felt the fireworks! And those feelings lasted about two days. After then, guess what happened? It became old and boring! Now, I needed to have my arm around her while we walked. The fireworks came back . . . for about two days. Then, guess what? You got it. Fireworks gone! Soon it was a kiss on the cheek, then a kiss on the mouth! Do you see the progression here?

It's never stagnant. (Not to say that those things were wrong, but if you follow the progression, they only led to one thing—maybe not immediately, but you get what I mean, right?)

This principle is applicable for many areas of life not just purity. Did you know that in the 1930s sodas were sold in six-ounce bottles? For years, six ounces was enough. People drank one bottle and were satisfied. But then in 1955, they launched a "King Size" 10-ounce and 12-ounce bottle. The 1960s brought out the 16-ounce. Then, the 21-ounce in 1974! And what happened in 1990? The convenience store 7-11 launched the Big Gulp—40 ounces in one cup! Wow! But it gets better. Today you can get a 64-ounce *Double Gulp*! That's over 10 times larger than what was normal at the beginning. That's not a cup; that's a small pond!

There's something about our culture that loves to push the limits. Why is this important to you? Because your faith is alive! Basically, you're either growing stronger and pushing towards God or growing weaker and falling away. Believe it or not, with

God *it is possible* to stay pure and avoid the sexual traps that are out there. The problem is, sin is fun. Straight up. If it wasn't, it wouldn't be so tempting! However, what's never shown in your favorite songs, shows, or movies is the consequences of sin. I tell young people all the time, "You will miss out when you live for God. That's right, you'll miss out on heartbreak, wasted time, STD's, unwanted pregnancies, and more!"

The problem is, sin is fun. Straight up. If it wasn't, it wouldn't be so tempting!

Those are worth missing. Remember this, sin will always take you further than you're willing to go, keep you longer than you're willing to stay, and cost you more than you're willing to pay.

WINNING THE BATTLE

The struggle of purity is real, so let's get down to how to win it. Here are four keys to victory against this battle.

#1

UNDERSTAND THAT PURITY IS A JOURNEY

It doesn't matter if you've read the Bible 50 times and in seven different languages, you'll never arrive at a place where you are "there." It's like graduating high school. When you graduate, you think, *I made it! It's over!* In reality, it's not over but just beginning! The life of purity works the same way.

Living in purity is not a spiritual diploma that blocks you from the temptations of the world. Instead, it's a decision to live a life in obedience to God with a *daily* commitment. Get this in your mind: Purity is a journey, not a destination.

I know so many young people who thought getting married was the point when God was going to somehow magically wipe away their lust, bad habits, and desire to look at other people. They were shocked when they found themselves participating in their same behavior as before they were married. One thing led to another and just like that, they were divorced and hurt. The reality is, we still live in a broken, fallen world. We have to grow our faith, and there is always work to be done.

Trust God that His ways always work best.

How do you grow stronger in the fight for purity? By building good habits. Even then, it's a daily decision that rests solely in your hands. Always remember that the highway called purity has many enticing exits. When you decide to live on this road, you will be drawn to jump off many times. Things may look good from the road; but in the end, it's not worth it. Trust God that His ways always work best.

It's your choice to drive this road. When you do, drive on and don't look back!

#2

SEEK GOD FERVENTLY

Key word here: *fervently*. To do something with fervor means to do it with intense passion. Passion makes a big difference in everything you do.

I remember one time in an Oakland Raiders team meeting room, there was a message on a screen that said, "Do it with passion or don't do it at all!" Throughout my life, I've seen the correlation between people who do things with passion and people who don't. The results don't even compare. King David is a great example. Look at his passion and the intensity of his hunger concerning his pursuit for God:

> *"O God, You are my God; early will I seek You; my soul thirsts for You; my flesh longs for You; in a dry and thirsty land, where there is no water."*[2]

Seeking God daily with this intense passion and making Him a priority in your life will help you stay on the highway of purity. Remember, this is the same David who killed the giant Goliath. Later, he grows up and becomes king. The story goes on to say that during a certain time of war, King David sent his mighty men to battle but decided to stay back himself. The Bible doesn't give a reason for his decision. Somehow, I believe, he lost his passion. That decision eventually put him in a very difficult position.

One of the best ways to live a life of purity is to eliminate the opportunity to fail.

While the men of Israel were out fighting their enemy, David encounters a lady bathing on the rooftop next door. (Yes, that's in the Bible!) The battle in his heart then began. No one was around. His mighty men and best friends were all at war. So, what does the king do? He sends for the lady—a married woman—and has an affair with her. To make matters worse, she gets pregnant! But it doesn't stop there. To cover up his sin, David orders her husband to the front lines where he was eventually killed in battle.

This is what happens when someone loses their passion for God!

Eventually, David's sin caught up with him, and he was confronted by a prophet named Nathan. Once called out, David repented and turned back to God. This was a good ending to a horrible series of bad choices with lifelong consequences.

Passion is the key. As you daily seek God with all your heart, it will build your purpose, identity, and help you to not lose momentum. Remember this: Your daily *moments* with God will give you the *momentum* to continually seek Him. As you stay faithful, your life then turns into a *movement* that God uses to impact the world!

#3

CREATE BOUNDARIES FOR YOURSELF

One of the best ways to live a life of purity is to eliminate the opportunity to fail. You have to win this fight before it even begins! The Bible says it like this:

> *"And do this, knowing the time, that now it is high time to awake out of sleep; for now our salvation is nearer than when we first believed. The night is far spent, the day is at hand. Therefore let us cast off the works of darkness, and let us put on the armor of light. Let us walk properly, as in the day, not in revelry and drunkenness, not in lewdness and lust, not in strife and envy. But put on the Lord Jesus Christ, and make no provision for the flesh, to fulfill its lusts."*[3]

Here are some boundaries that have worked for me and some young people I have mentored. These aren't the only ones. There are many more. I pray that you seek God, listen to His voice, and obey. I pray this help you.

Boundary #1: Do Not Avoid Red Flags

Newsflash: You cannot change people! You can only change yourself. Some relationship red flags are habits, you see. Things like: Do they have a job? Are they responsible? What are the things they listen to and watch? How do they treat people? Then, there's their friends, stuff on their social media profiles, past relationships, etc. Of course, people always promise to change. But a great rule of thumb is this: Date *patterns*, not *promises.*

Boundary #2: No God, No Go!

You would think this would be a given, but it's not. So many good, God-loving, Christian young people throw away their pursuit of purity with someone they knew wasn't right for them from the very beginning. The bottom line is this: If they're not in love with God, then they shouldn't even be an option!

Believe it or not, I do know people who have built relationships with others who weren't walking with God, and they ended up getting married and are doing very well. Those stories are few and very far between. My encouragement is for you to hear from God and consult those around you who can give you wisdom.

Having a strong, authentic relationship with Christ is the right foundation on which to build a relationship—and just simply going to church won't cut it! Remember that going to church doesn't make someone a Christian any more than walking into a garage makes them a car!

No, are they walking with Jesus daily? Do they have a passion for what God has for their life? If your end goal is marriage, then you'll need a strong connection to God to make a strong and effective marriage. The life of a Christian is one of faith, generosity, prayer, serving your local church, and your community. Being connected to someone with no relationship with Christ will make it very difficult to have a thriving relationship.

Boundary #3: Know Yourself

Before jumping into a new relationship, ask yourself, "Am I ready for this?" Be honest. A great way to know is how you ended your last one. How you leave one is how you will enter another. Take time to get healed. Do not jump into the next thing without smart counsel.

Boundary #4: Set Limits

Hanging out with someone one-on-one should be in public, not in private. Try to hang with others in restaurants or malls, so you truly get to know the person. Being alone in private can most often put your emotions into overdrive. This leads to situations that open the door to physical activity. Physical attraction is easy, but don't fall in love with the outside. Get to know the whole person, which starts on the inside.

This also applies to talking, texting, or chatting on social media platforms. Set a time to cut it off and stick with it.

Boundary #5: Always Keep Jesus First

No matter how perfect or dreamy they may be, never make this person your whole world! Only one person has the right to hold that spot—Jesus. When you give away too much time to this person, you will hurt in other areas like school, family, friends, church, and even your training, practices, and competitions. It's about making priorities.

#4
FIND REAL ACCOUNTABILITY

When most people hear the word, "accountability," they think this is to make sure they live a boring, miserable life! But that's not true. Accountability can be one of your best tools in the battle to live pure. You were never meant to fight this war alone. You were created for community—to be surrounded by people who will help, stand with, and fight for you. Here are a few tips on finding the right accountability partner.

Find someone who's older than you, someone you respect who loves God, who is committed to being there for you, and who you can be completely honest with.

Give this person permission to talk about the hard stuff—the things you probably wouldn't talk about to many others. Many times, this person can be your youth pastor, church leader, coach, dad, or mentor. Here's the deal. You must seek them out. Most of these people are very busy and won't come looking for you, but I've learned that if you'll ask God, He will bring those people around. When He does, then you have to ask.

Accountability is another form of discipleship. I keep hearing about how our world is having a "millennial" or "youth" problem. I love how one of my dear friends put it: "We don't have a millennial problem; we have a discipleship problem." Don't be afraid to ask. Don't be afraid to open up. Most of these amazing people would be honored to make time and bring you into their world. It's the way Jesus meant it to be.

This topic is so personal. It's one that your enemy would love for you to keep in the dark and convince you that you can win on your own. Would you take a moment and ask God's Holy Spirit to speak to you? You may need forgiveness right now and God is ready to give it to you. Maybe you have been carrying shame and guilt and God is asking you right now to let Him take it from you.

Understand this: First of all, you are not disqualified to be used by God! God doesn't call the qualified; He qualifies the called. The Bible says, *"If we confess our sins, He is faithful and just and will FORGIVE us our sins and PURIFY us from all unrighteousness."*[4] Confession to God brings forgiveness.

Secondly, you need to confess your sin to someone who can be a mentor/pastor to you. Watch this: *"Therefore confess your sins to each other and pray for each other so that you may be HEALED . . .,"*[5] Confession vertically (to God) brings forgiveness; confession horizontally (to a mentor) brings healing and freedom. You can do this!

GAME CHANGER

KENYON COLEMAN

PROFESSIONAL FOOTBALL PLAYER

In 2002, Oakland drafted a defensive lineman from UCLA named Kenyon Coleman. I had no idea that this 6'5" almost 300-pound guy would become one of my great friends in life. Kenyon stood out immediately as a rookie not because of his play, but because of his love for God and passion to share his faith. He played an incredible 11 seasons as a professional football player but is remembered by most for his contagious faith in Jesus. I sat down with him at a coffee shop he owns and we talked about this tough topic of purity. Here's what he had to say:

> *If I'm being honest, the topic of a life of purity scared the heck out of me. As an athlete at UCLA getting ready to turn pro in the League, I was invited to every party, and I drew a lot of attention. In my college*

years, I took my sport and education seriously, but it was then when I really wanted to grow in my relationship with God, as well. I started feeling this calling and purpose for my life that was bigger than me. It had to do with who I was and who I was becoming.

Staying pure was tough. Temptation was everywhere. My tight schedule helped me to stay focused, which made my hunger for God begin to grow. I would see guys living that lifestyle and pursuing those choices, but I stayed focused. It paid off when I got drafted by the Oakland Raiders in the fifth round of the 2002 draft! Just like that, I was single, a pro-football player, and I had money. I immediately began to discover that there's a culture in the pros that says, "Hey, you made it. Enjoy it all. God will forgive you!" Like we get a pass to live life how we want and not worry about consequences. That's not reality.

While at UCLA, I met a gymnast named Katie. We were friends but never really connected because of our rigorous schedules. In my rookie year with the Raiders, a mutual friend finally connected us. She was beautiful, funny, smart, and she was pursuing God! Before we began hanging out and getting to know each other, we set strict boundaries to not date and get physical. But the more we hung out, the more the battle in our minds and hearts got tougher and tougher. We finally gave in and kissed. Then, we gave into more and more. One night, we got a scare when we thought Katie was pregnant. We knew we loved each other and that marriage was our goal, so with much prayer and counsel from our pastor, we got married three weeks later with a few witnesses.

I worked my tail off to be my best on the field and off. Off the field, I started meeting with spiritual leaders like my chaplains, reading my Bible and Christian books daily, and praying. Also, any opportunity I had to serve the local church or community, I was there. My faith and connection with God began to grow. Katie and I began to feel a true transformation from deep within. We were re-born. I began hearing God's voice much clearer, and I discovered my spiritual gifts. I just loved sharing God's redemptive love to everyone. It would've been easy for football to have become my identity, but I chose to take this stand instead: I am a Christian who just so happens to play professional football.

I'm grateful to have played 12 seasons in the national league with five different teams—twice with Dallas. Every team and every locker room was different, but the temptations were always the same, always there. Some locker rooms literally had boxes of porn DVD's laying around for whoever. Some guys would take those and watch them on flights heading to away games. Then, once we were at our hotel, guys would meet up with girls and take them to their rooms or go out—not just single guys; married ones, too! It broke my heart to see guys go down that road. All this time, my teammates knew my stand, as I had made it clear the road I was on.

Here's what I learned early on in my pro career. In the church world, we typically teach restraint instead of the transformation of the mind. Don't get me wrong, boundaries are great, but we need to go deeper for victory! If you don't have a mental transformation, you'll find a way to break boundaries. One of the biggest transformations for me was that if I wanted to find a woman of God, I had to be a man of God.

Stephen Arterburn's amazing book, Every Man's Battle, had a huge impact on me. The book was full of countless stories of Christian men with private struggles and the lives impacted by their failures. I didn't want to end up like that. Reading it helped me to magnify the consequences of my decisions, and value my future for myself and those around me. I learned that we can't just conceive thoughts of lust and then . . . POOF! . . . just abort them. It doesn't work that way. One great example in the Bible was how Samson was lured by lust only to lose everything God entrusted to Him. These stories and biblical examples all gave me a passion to lead other guys in a different way of living.

One way I led my teammates was by taking out the porn in our locker room. One had porn in the bathroom stalls. So, what did I do? Threw them all out and replaced them with Christian books! Guys would come and ask me, "Why are you so strict?" I would say, "I won't give up my daily blessings." Those blessings are my connection with God and my connection with my wife and kids.

No matter if you're an athlete or not, the tests and trials of purity will always be there. My encouragement to you today is that if you've made mistakes or choices that you wish you could take back, ask God for forgiveness. Confess those wrongs and receive God's forgiveness and mercy. Then, start on the highway of purity and don't get off of it. It's worth it! If you're struggling with private things, bring them to the light with a trusted mentor or pastor. The devil wants nothing more than to keep all that hidden in the dark so you can't experience real transformation and freedom.

The time is now. Let God use your life and watch others be impacted forever. ➽

6

THE BATTLE FOR YOUR GIFTS

One of my favorite passages in the Bible is found in the Old Testament. It's where God is calling Moses to be the leader of His people, and to march them out of 400 years of slavery. Now, you would think that when God is asking him to be such a hero, Moses would have jumped at the opportunity. But he didn't. Instead, he offered God every excuse he could think of as to why he was not qualified. Check out part of this conversation:

> *"But Moses protested again, 'What if they won't believe me or listen to me? What if they say, "The Lord never appeared to you?"' Then the Lord asked him, 'What is that in your hand?' 'A shepherd's staff,' Moses replied. 'Throw it down on the ground,' the Lord told him. So Moses threw down the staff, and it turned into a snake! Moses jumped back."*[1]

Let's focus on that question, "What is in your hand?" For Moses, it was his staff. The staff that fought off animals attacking his sheep, the staff that kept his sheep in line, and the staff that gave him strength and assistance as he walked. I wonder if Moses ever wanted a different staff? A better or newer one? God could've used anything He wanted, but He chose the thing that had been with Moses the whole time. He chose what was already in his hand!

Here's one thing to always remember: God always does things on purpose and for a purpose. In Moses' hands, that staff was just a piece of wood; but in God's hands, it became a weapon that would be used to free His people. The same is true today. Whatever is in your hands will always be ordinary. But in the hands of God, it becomes extraordinary! A baseball that cost $25 in my hands is worth $25, but in the hands of Clayton Kershaw, it's worth millions. A 9-inch steel nail in my hands is worth about 45 cents; however, that same nail in the hands of our Savior, Jesus, is worth all the sins of the world! Natural things *always* become supernatural in the hands of our God. We are the natural—God is the super.

God always does things on purpose and for a purpose.

When you place your little in God's hands, it becomes great!

The Bible is full of such stories. One that stands out is the little boy who brought the food that he had (actually it was two fish and five loaves of bread) to this big meeting where Jesus was preaching. Thousands were there and they were hungry! Jesus was looking for something to multiply, so the boy gave up what was in his hands. And what happened? God multiplied it and fed everyone there! Here's the crazier thing. The Bible says that after everyone had eaten, there were still baskets full of food left over! Imagine that for a second. This young boy left home with two fish and five loaves of bread but came back with a basket full of bread and fish! That's the way God works. You always get more than you came for. Put your gift right back in the hands of God and let Him do great things as He leads you.

WHO'S NEXT?

One of the most popular TV commercials played over the last few years ends with this question, "What's in your wallet?" The question I want to ask you is, "What's in your hand?" What do you have, right now, that God can add His *super* to your *natural*?

Did you know that everyone is born with over 300 abilities and gifts? That includes you! You have numerous gifts and talents, but there's usually one or two that stick out above all the others. Maybe you can sing, preach, write, teach, play a sport, dance, design, etc. There are gifts placed in you by God—and that's not all. There's also a battle for your gifts.

So many of today's celebrities have amazing gifts but use them for themselves. Can you imagine if Beyonce or Drake would have used their gifts for God's purposes instead of their own? I was so excited to see God get a hold of Kanye West! Here is one of music's leading voices—who admits to singing about alcohol, partying, and girls—but now is on a mission to tell everyone about Jesus. It's incredible. His album, *Jesus is King*, soared to the top of the charts, and his concerts with his gospel choir have been telling millions about Jesus.

Kanye is a Culture Changer. My question is, "Who will be the next major influencer to start using their gifts for God? It just might be you! Let's not be quick to judge celebrities and influencers, but be quick to pray for them. God may be working on them and we have no idea. Let's believe God to win as many as possible into God's kingdom.

PUT THEM TO WORK

One of the most interesting parts of Moses' story was when God told him to take his staff and lay it down. When he did, God did a miracle with it. What if Moses would have picked it up? It would have died and returned to normal. It's still the same. Every time you take back what God has asked you to give Him and use it for your own glory and fame, it will die. But, when you use what's in your hand for God, He will always use it for supernatural impact.

What would it look like if you used your gifts, ideas, and talents for God? I want you to stop right here, right now, and ask God, "Lord, how can I use what's in my hands for Your glory and purpose?" One of my spiritual influences always ended every church service by asking his congregation, "What is the Holy Spirit telling you?" That's exactly what I'm asking you now. I honestly believe He's already speaking to your spirit. Listen, and then obey.

As I said before, there is a battle raging for every Culture Changer's gifts. Here are three tips on how to win that war:

#1
BE CONFIDENT IN YOUR GIFTS

They are just that—gifts. Be confident and work your gift, sharpen your gift, and use your gift for God. When you do, confidence will begin to rise. Don't wait! Your gift is *needed.*

I believe football is one of the most incredible examples of unity and teamwork. It's a group of people from different backgrounds and talents all coming together for a greater goal. The team has to work together to obtain something they could not by themselves. The running back needs the lineman to use their incredible skills to move another huge, strong individuals out of the way. The players depend on each other. It's the same in the game of life. We all need each other.

I thank God for my friends at church who lead us in worship, run the cameras, edit the videos, and work in the parking lot every week. I'm thankful for my pastor who teaches us and for the teachers who lead my kids in their classes. You see, not only does the world need your gift, but I'm going to be bolder and say that people's destinies are waiting to be impacted by your gift! I know. I was one of them.

At 19 years old, I came to a church service broken, lost, and hurting. The lady who was a guest speaker that day had the spiritual gifts of prophecy and word of knowledge. (You can find those in 1 Corinthians 12:8.) As she came up to speak, she said, "Where is that young man with the cross necklace I passed in the hallway?" It was me. I stood up and she then began to say stuff I had never shared with anyone. She said, "The Lord showed me your mom passed and your dad has not been in your life. You have a call of God on your life and He is going to use you to touch thousands. You will travel and share the gospel of Jesus everywhere." She went on and prayed over me. I was weeping like a baby. Then, I felt an intense heat come over me. I had never been drunk or high in my life, so it was something I had never experienced. It was God.

That moment forever shifted me. It was the moment I stopped running from God and said, "Okay, God, I'm yours. Whatever You want, let's go." That day was June 22, and I still celebrate that day every year.

Think about that for a second. That moment changed my entire future—my future marriage, my kids, my ministry, even my bloodline. Literally, everything about me was changed forever. Now, what if this lady wasn't confident that the Lord had spoken to her? What if she had listened to doubt or fear and not called me out? I'm sure both were present at that moment. My life would be way different.

That was me and the lady preacher. But, what about you? What if God wants you to write the next song that helps people encounter God in their worship? Or direct a film that helps the visual of the Bible appear in a live movie? What if your paintings could inspire and motivate others? What if the books you write help heal and bless people? It's never too early to start. Don't wait. Develop and use your gifts as much as you can right now. God gave them to you for you and others to experience Him.

#2

BE THANKFUL FOR YOUR GIFTS

Think about what this world would like if we all had the same gifts. Life would be so boring! In God's greatness, He created us all so unique but we're working in unity to win in this thing called life. Here's the good news: You are part of His master plan! For that, you should be thankful.

When you are thankful, you begin to enjoy the ride and the journey God has put you on. Thankfulness gives you peace, and it keeps you humble. Don't wait for the "perfect situation" to come around before you're thankful. For example, don't say, "If I could just use my gift on TV or in front of large crowds, then I'd be thankful!" This type of attitude will cause life to pass you by, leaving you filled with jealousy and a sense of unfulfillment.

When you are thankful, you begin to enjoy the ride and the journey God has put you on.

Look what that Bible says about this:

"Always be joyful. Never stop praying. Be thankful in all circumstances, for this is God's will for you who are in Christ Jesus."[2]

It's not always easy to have a thankful heart, but when you do, you please the Lord's heart and your enemy is defeated. Thankfulness is easy when things are going right, but a lot harder when things are going rough. Being thankful for your gifts brings contentment. It will help you focus and use your gifts with confidence.

#3
DON'T COMPARE YOUR GIFTS

Everybody has unique gifts. Comparing what you have with others will kill your joy and make you question what God has given you. It can also make you ungrateful and resentful. Neither of these are beneficial to your life.

When I was in Bible college, it seemed like everyone could play an instrument or sing amazingly well. Some could do both! I battled this every day as I watched my peers sing and play in daily chapel services. Some of them were really good and my desire to be like them was always in my face. I wanted to sing so badly that I started taking lessons. Some friends tried to help and I got decent to where I could at least hold a tune, but that definitely wasn't my gift. I even watched YouTube videos on how to play the piano. Again, music just wasn't my gift.

My gift is the ability to communicate, speak, motivate, and make the Bible relevant to everyday people. Here's what I learned: God isn't looking for someone who has it all; He's looking for someone who's willing to surrender it all. You see, it's not about your *abilities*; it's about your *availability*! Can you trust God enough to believe He didn't make a mistake with you, that He wants to use you in the fullness of how He created you with every gift, ability, and talent?

God isn't looking for someone who has it all;

He's looking for someone who's willing to surrender it all.

If you want to discover your calling in life, there are two big clues God has given you: (1.) What's in your hand and (2.) what's in your heart. What talent do you have and what are you crazy passionate about? Your life's calling will always be centered around these two things. When you follow these and give them to God, you will never hate your job and feel stuck.

Let me encourage you, God is waiting. The time is now. Tomorrow is never guaranteed. Don't wait another day. Seek Him now and then step out in obedience and faith!

You will not be disappointed.

2-MINUTE DRILL

There was a lie that you believed about you and your gifts/abilities. What was it? Now take that lie and literally expose it as a lie. Next, replace it with a truth you learned in this chapter. I want you to take that truth and write it down on something you can put up on your door or desk, somewhere you will see it everyday. Begin to speak and agree with that truth every morning before you head off to start your day! Look for ways you can use your gift for God. The easiest way is to see what's happening in your local church or even campus. Serve God with your gift! Keep speaking it until you believe it and are walking in it. Make it a daily affirmation. Commit to develop your gifts and honor God with them as He leads you.

GAME CHANGER

ERVIN WILSON

MUSICIAN & SINGER / SONGWRITER

Some of my favorite memories are serving as a youth pastor in San Jose, CA. Our youth group was called 2Twenty2, which was based on 2 Timothy 2:22. We saw God move in so many ways. Those students became etched in my heart forever. One student always stuck out to me—Ervin Wilson. He has a really cool journey about understanding his gifts and using them for the Lord. Ervin started in our group as a sixth grader, and today he's a young adult following the call of God on his life. I asked him to share his story.

> *Before I was 15 years old, I didn't know what to do with my life. I tended to enjoy and endure whatever came out of my everyday experience. No purpose. Both my parents are pastors, so I was deeply rooted in my church in San Jose, CA. There came a moment where for months, leaders in my youth group would bring up the idea of singing and serving on the worship team. They saw a gift in me that I definitely did not see.*
>
> *Back then I was not a fan of singing or being on a stage in front of people. I actually thought it was corny in a way. But the leaders wouldn't stop asking me about it. To be honest, my heart started changing, but I was too afraid to step out. Then I decided to try out to play drums for the team. I figured that if I at least made it, then people would stop bothering me about it!*
>
> *My audition went well and I made the team! A few months later, someone brought up the idea for me to try out as a singer. They said if I didn't like it, I'd never have to do it again. So, I agreed. Like my first audition, I was super nervous and fearful but decided to do it just so the leaders would stop jumping my case about it. Nothing could have prepared me for what I would experience that Sunday morning. I wasn't just happy; I was full of joy! It was supernatural. I felt free worshipping on the stage, so much so that I never went back to playing drums!*
>
> *Entering into my late teens, my love for music and ministering through it grew. It came naturally to me. Writing songs and making music just started flowing. I began to realize that this was the reason why God put*

me on this earth. This was my gift. No longer did I need to search or question; it was burning in my heart.

As I kept growing in my faith, God began giving me visions of going to new places and traveling all around the world as an artist who made music for His Kingdom. God used His people to help encourage me and see things I didn't see in myself. Stepping out in faith meant I had to conquer the fear. When I did, I found joy and purpose!

Holding true to the promises of God has been the thing that has kept me going. Everything that God has promised, He will fulfill! It takes me being totally surrendered to God and His will. I have fully realized that God can take my little and make it great.

Today, I continue to lead worship at my local church while releasing a new, authentic form of music that connects people to God and their purpose. It's all for God and I trust that He will do everything He wants with me. I thank God for everything that He's doing and for what He will continue to do as He brings me more into my purpose!

When learning to walk in your gifts and talents, trust God to give you peace in your storm. Listen to those God has placed around you—the people who see things in you that you can't. Also, stay connected to your church and the community of faith. This is so important. ➽

7

THE BATTLE FOR APPROVAL

Roger Bannister was the first man in the world to run a mile under four minutes in May 1954. It was unthinkable at the time. The very next month, Australian John Landy broke that record by 1.4 seconds. In August 1954, the two fastest mile runners in the world met for a historic race at the British Empire Games in Vancouver, Canada. The race was dubbed "The miracle mile," "The race of the century," and "The dream race." The race started with Bannister and Landy neck and neck. As they turned for the last lap, Landy was in the lead and looked certain to win. But as he neared the finish line, Landy lost focus and allowed his mind to wonder about Bannister's position. Unable to stand the strain, he finally looked back over his shoulder. When he did, Landy broke his stride and Bannister passed him to break the tape and win the race!

What is it about wanting to look over at others running our same race? Personally, I constantly struggled with this for years. I was always looking for other people's approval, comparing myself and tracking with what others were doing. A lot of it had to do with my family situation at home. With the rise of social media, comparing my worst days to everyone else's best posts was so dejecting. It's what's called the Battle of Approval—a battle every Culture Changer must face . . . and must win.

ONLY ONE

Here's a major problem with this battle: We tend to seek the approval of others more than being content with God's approval! It's nothing new. The Apostle Paul dealt with this same issue back in the New Testament days. Look what he wrote:

> *"Am I now trying to win the approval of human beings or of God? Or am I trying to please people? If I were still trying to please people, I would not be a servant of Christ."*[1]

Stop trying to win the approval of people who could walk out of your life in a heartbeat.

I already mentioned the lure of social media. Let me expand on it a little. It's no secret that social media feeds and posts dominate so many people's lives, especially young people. While it can keep you connected and in-the-know about so many things, social media can also bury you. Be careful scrolling and looking at people's posts. Why? Because nobody EVER posts their worst moments, their worst look, or their worst situations! You are only seeing people at their best. So, when you start comparing your worst to their best, you lose—at least, in your mind.

Statistics are proving that more time spent on social media means lower self-esteem and higher cases of depression. Don't fall into this trap. Your value doesn't come from "Likes," "Followers," or shares; it comes from what God was willing to pay for you! The Bible clearly says it:

> *"For God so loved the world that He gave His only begotten Son, that whoever believes in Him should not perish but have everlasting life."*[2]

Look at that. God gave *everything* for you. His everything is way more than anyone you can ever have. Nothing else even comes close at second place. That makes you the most valuable thing on the planet! And every day, God pursues you and desires to connect with you, to heal you, and to empower you. What person on this earth can match that? No one! Stop trying to win the approval of people who could walk out of your life in a heartbeat. I've been on the wrong end of that, and it's no fun. There's only one approval to seek: the One who has already given everything to you!

Statistics are proving that more time spent on social media means lower self-esteem and higher cases of depression.

TWO KEYS

Staying focused on God's approval can be difficult. Here are two keys to help:

#1

STAY THANKFUL

I like to say that being thankful to God is being *full* of *thanks*. One of the things I do with my kids every night before bed is to have them share five things from the day that they're thankful for. There's something about being thankful that helps you realize the bigger picture and brings contentment and peace. If you're having a hard time being thankful, start with these two things.

- **Be thankful for what God has already done.** Someone once told me, "Want the things you have, not the things you don't have!" I promise that if you think about that, you'll turn this list into a worship session. From the times He's come through for you to the times you've heard His voice to the day you encountered Him for the first time—be thankful! How about all the stuff God shielded you from that you didn't even see or know about? The bad accident you passed on the road could have killed you, the relationship that could have destroyed you, the sickness that could have taken you out. Man, there are so many things to be thankful for. You just have to start acknowledging what they are.

- **Be thankful for things He's going to do.** When you start thanking Him for the things He's already done, it will build your faith to thank Him for what He's going to do. The Bible says that God is able to do far more than you can even think or imagine.[3] There are no limits for God. If you can dream it, God can go beyond it! That's great news. When you live a life of thankfulness, it helps to keep your eyes off of what others say and keep your eyes on Jesus.

#2

FIND THE RIGHT CIRCLE

I once heard a pastor say something that has stuck with me for years. He said, "To be successful, go where you're celebrated and not just tolerated." If you feel like you're losing the Battle of Approval, the first question to ask yourself is, "Who's surrounding me?" I'm not talking about followers or popularity, but the people in your inner circle. Who are they? What are they like? Do they push you to be great? Are they cheering you on even when you have setbacks or failures? That circle can make you or break you.

It's been said many times that if you show me your friends, I'll show you your future. That is so true. Friends are so important. Well, let me say it another way—*good* friends are important! Good friends are the ones God uses to bring affirmation, love, and even correction into your life. Unfortunately, many people have abused that in families, churches, and Christian circles. But I am living proof that it works. I'm grateful for the amazing circle of good friends in my life, the ones who constantly push me towards God and hold me accountable. Heck, I finished this book because my pastor asked me, "Chris, what has God told you to do that you haven't finished yet?" Ouch! I'm glad he pushed me.

Be friendly to all; be friends to few.

When you surround yourself with good, godly friends, they will help you be all God has called you to be. This will build your heart to be joyful, and you will enjoy God's approval for your life!

2-MINUTE DRILL

Ok, moment of truth. What areas in your life are you seeking man's approval for instead of God's? Are you surrounded by people who help push you towards God? You don't need a huge crew of friends; you really only need one or two who you can do life with. I have this saying: Be friendly to all, be friends to few! Part of attracting the right people is learning to be the right person! Are you a good friend? One worth pursuing? Quiet yourself and ask God two things: (1.) to show you areas not surrendered to Him and (2.) to bring you godly friendships. Anytime you hear God speak, obedience is key. It does you no good to be able to hear God, if you won't obey. That's how you come to know Him and walk in His purposes.

GAME CHANGER

JUSTIN FORSETT

PRO BOWL RUNNING BACK

One of my favorite people on the planet is Justin Forsett. He's a guy whose work ethic, confidence, and love for God are crazy inspiring. Most guys have a hard time adjusting to life after a professional football career, but not Justin. He has been thriving after retirement. Along with some teammates from college, Justin started a company called Hustle Clean. It's now in every Target store in the country! He even had an opportunity to pitch his business on the show *Shark Tank*. What makes Justin stand out is how focused he is on pleasing the ultimate coach, Jesus Christ, and not worrying about the crowd in the stands.

You would think that having incredible stats as a running back and leading your high school football team to back-to-back state titles would get some amazing attention and recognition. What do you do when you have the talent, stats, and video footage to back it up, but you don't have the size for anyone to take you seriously?

That is exactly my story.

Growing up in a small Florida town, I began dreaming about playing professional football in the League. Of course, everyone always told me what I couldn't do. Throughout my life, I heard the same things over and over. "You're too small! You won't last!" So, I had to make a decision. Would their words be my reality or would I use them as fuel for motivation? If I had listened to the crowd and the haters, I definitely would not have had a 9-year career in the League and played in the Pro Bowl.

Because I was smaller, I never took a day off—not even Sundays. If I couldn't have the size advantage, then I'd work harder to be quicker, smarter, and faster than everyone else. My family eventually moved to Texas for a better opportunity. The kids were bigger and the competition was fierce, but that only motivated me more.

My dad was a pastor, so I grew up learning about God. I knew with Him, hard work, and dedication, great things could happen. I grew to about 5'8" in high school and weighed 185 pounds. I flourished and had an incredible high school career, yet I was only rated as a two-star recruit. There were no scholarship offers and no college recruiters calling. I was very disappointed.

Then it happened.

Notre Dame called and wanted to meet with me. They were willing to give me a scholarship and a chance! I was so excited. But two days before National Signing Day, they called back and said, "We don't need you anymore." It was devastating, embarrassing, and a blow to my dreams.

A little while later, my break came just like I believed. Cal Berkeley called and offered me a scholarship and a chance to play. Little did I know the great players I would have the opportunity to play with there. Guys like Marshawn Lynch, Aaron Rodgers, and Desean Jackson. I was living my dream.

It didn't take long for me to come to this conclusion: At every level, you have to decide to play for an audi-

ence of one—God. I've had the opportunity to play in front of thousands of fans, but you can't get caught up in that. Over my nine-year career, I played with seven teams. That means I got fired way more than I would have liked, but I never quit and never lost sight of what matters. Sure, it hurts to be let go, for someone to say, "I'm sorry, you're just not good enough." Everybody goes through those tough times. The crowd will even boo you, but there's someone who believes in you and will be there to help you every step of the way.

Don't give up. Don't give in. Keep working because it's going to pay off. I can tell you, it's worth it!

8

THE BATTLE FOR FORGIVENESS

Listen to this statement: Hurt people, hurt people. So many people ask questions like, "Why do bad things happen?" or "Why is there so much pain and evil in the world?" I've learned that it comes down to one thing—sin. Like it or not, we live in a broken world, and it will stay broken until Jesus returns.

When Adam and Eve sinned in the Garden of Eden, it caused a string of consequences that everyone since then has had to deal with. Because of sin, bad things happen. Our fallen nature is why you don't have to teach little kids how to be sneaky and do bad things. It's in them. We have to teach them how to do good things! That's the power of sin.

Over the years, I've heard so many stories from young people all across the world of the things they have gone through. It never ceases to blow my mind how many teenagers have been raped, abused, neglected, abandoned, and bullied—not to mention those who have had to live with the horrors of divorce, racism, and mistreatment. The most amazing thing is how many have come through it and have overcome through God's grace.

That's the power of the cross!

When people go through bad things, one of the hardest challenges is forgiving the ones who caused the pain.

When people go through bad things, one of the hardest challenges is forgiving the ones who caused the pain. True forgiveness isn't easy, but it's necessary to live your life to the fullest. This is exactly why Jesus challenges us to forgive those who have wronged us not once, not seven times, not 70 times, but 490 times! I heard a pastor put it this way, "Forgiveness isn't something you pursue, it's something you possess!" and you already have it *in* Christ.

MY STORY

I have had many moments in my life when I needed to forgive and also when I needed to be forgiven. One of these times happened soon after I accepted Jesus as my Lord and Savior and placed my faith in Him.

I was so excited about my new life in Christ. I had a new identity and was experiencing the joy of being fully forgiven for *all* my sin! The night I placed my faith in Christ, the preacher prophesied over me and said that I would speak to thousands and travel the world! (Remember that story?) Well, I was like, "Ok,

God. Let's go!" But before all that cool stuff could take place, something had to happen first—something I wasn't quite ready for.

My first assignment from the Lord wasn't to preach to thousands. Quite the opposite. The first thing I ever heard God speak to me was, "Chris, you need to forgive someone who has hurt you deeply. I have forgiven you. Now, go and forgive your dad!" I can tell you, that wasn't on my radar at all! I was like, "Wait, this is what You want me to do first? This isn't being in front of thousands. This isn't getting on planes, traveling to cool places, staying in great hotels." You see, I had all these ideas of what I thought was important, but God said, "No, you got it twisted. This journey is filled with hard and tough assignments that will stretch you and mold you!"

When I was three years old, my father divorced my mother and left her for another woman. That decision, whether he knew it or not, would affect not only my life, but my future family's life, as well. (Never forget, your choices will always affect more than just you.) My mom did the best she could to raise me solo. My dad tried his best to see me, but I was rebellious from trying to sort out all of the hurt. So, I grew up abandoned, upset, and angered. My whole foundation was unstable.

I was 19 years old when God spoke to me about forgiving my father. That's 16 years after he left us. Honestly, I didn't feel like he deserved forgiveness. More than that, I felt like he needed to apologize to me! It was then that I realized that my deep-seated unforgiveness had turned into bitterness. I asked my mentor what I should do. He encouraged me to be obedient to what God was speaking to my heart and shared with me this passage:

"For if you forgive other people when they sin against you, your heavenly Father will also forgive you. But if you do not forgive others their sins, your Father will not forgive your sins."[1]

Now, I knew what I had to do.

I prayed and prayed, asking God for the courage. Then, I did it. I picked up the phone and called my father. My mind had convinced me that this was going to be the hardest thing I had ever done up to this point in my life. I played out the scenario over and over in my head. I pictured the conversation going something like this:

"Hey Dad, it's Chris, your son. I just wanted to call and say that I'm sorr . . ."

"Son, stop. I'm sorry! Thank you for calling me."

That would've been nice, but it's not quite how it happened.

When I called and my father picked up, I started off by saying, "Dad, it's Chris, your son." He answers, "Chris, it's great to hear from you. I knew you'd call me someday!" Hold up. What? This isn't how it's supposed to go! In that moment, about 10,000 curse words flew through my mind that I wanted to say. But I felt God speak to my heart and say, "Chris, you can do this My way, or you can do it your way." I knew I needed to humble myself. I continued, "Dad, however you want to look at it, God brought us back together."

Our conversation continued with him asking if I was in college. I shared how I wanted to be in ministry, which he replied, "Son, you'll be poor like that. You can't support a family that way!" (Thanks for the encouragement!) I shared what God did in my life and how He completely changed me. Then, with a firm and sharp tone, he said, "Don't tell me about Jesus! I have co-workers sending me emails about Jesus, and I don't need to hear it!"

After our conversation, I felt so much joy. I felt such freedom now that this huge weight I had carried for years had been lifted off! It was the start of rebuilding our relationship! Today, we have a great relationship. My dad is not the same person as he was during that phone call. He Facetimes with my kids and even says, "God bless you, Son. I love you." I'm so glad that my first assignment wasn't speaking at a large church or firing up a pro sports team before a game, but instead forgiving my Dad.

Obedience paid off.

God doesn't always live up to our expectations, but He always lives up to His Word!

TAKE THE STEPS

Here's a lesson I learned through forgiving my Dad. God doesn't always live up to our *expectations*, but He always lives up to His *Word*! Placing expectations on how we think something should work out usually leads to hurt and frustration. God's Word says that He will always be with us, guide us, and strengthen us. His Word has the final say!

Maybe your parents divorced and you prayed that they would get back together, but it didn't happen. That caused frustration. Maybe you're a great athlete, thinking God would give you success on a professional level, but an early injury ended your sports career. Listen, we don't know the future, but we do know the One who holds the future. When you hear God, make sure it lines up with His Word.

In your journey, you will come to rough moments that will knock you down. It's called life! Then, you will have two choices: You can stay down or get up and keep walking with God. Forgiveness is one of those areas where you will be challenged to the core, but it also can release freedom into your life like nothing else.

Here are some key things to know about forgiveness.

- Forgiveness is a daily choice.
- Forgiveness is for you, not them.
- Forgiveness does not mean what happened was okay.
- Forgiveness is a commandment by God.
- Forgiveness does not mean you have to re-establish relationship.

This may sound harsh, but for me, there are some non-negotiables when it comes to parenting. In our family, we eat meals together, we go to church together, and we have rules in our house that aren't up for discussion. These are not suggestions, but it's the way we do it. God looks at forgiveness the same way—it's not a suggestion, an urging, or even good advice. It's a command and we must obey.

Let me set something straight that you may not understand. Many people think that to forgive someone means you have to re-establish relationship. This isn't the truth. Sometimes, you will, but these are two completely separate issues. The best advice is to guard your heart and don't allow unforgiveness to become bitterness. If you have a desire to punish or take revenge on someone, repent immediately. Let God deal with the offense, not you. Focus on today rather than the past. Let the offender off the hook! Declare God as judge over the person and the situation.

I'm sure you've heard the phrase, "Forgive and forget," many times. It sounds unrealistic, but it is possible. However, God gave me a different phrase that has helped me forgive on many occasions. Here it is: Forgive and *never* forget! What? Yes, you heard me right. Forgive and never forget. Never forget how God has fully forgiven you for *all* your sins! Did you catch that? When you remind yourself daily of all that God has done for you, it helps you to see others in the same light. Everyone is broken, just like you, and in need of a Savior and the forgiveness of God.

I've heard it said many times that harboring unforgiveness is like drinking poison and hoping that your enemy will die. The only one dying is you!

So, right now, do *you* need to forgive someone? Maybe it's a parent, sibling, leader, or co-worker. Of course, the number one person you may have to forgive is yourself! So, do it! Don't live another second of your life with unforgiveness. It's not worth it. The time to forgive is now. I had to do it. It wasn't easy, but the results are amazing. God wants you to be free today!

2-MINUTE DRILL

This is important. Not forgiving will have huge consequences that will echo throughout every area of your life and those in your life. Quiet yourself and ask God's help in your heart right now. Ask him to do the lifting, to do the work. Ok, are you ready to let some anger and hurt go? If so, here are some action steps for you:

- Share your pain with God and release it to Him. (Psalm 30:2)
- Forgive the offender and let God be the judge. (Romans 12:19)
- Bless the offender. This is the biggest proof you have forgiven them. (Romans 12:14)

GAME CHANGER

LINDSAY RORICK

FELLOWSHIP OF CHRISTIAN ATHLETES AREA REPRESENTATIVE

Working in the sports world, it's easy for me to connect with the guys. It was always a lot harder to try and impact the women's side of sports. As a man there's only so much I can do. I love speaking to our lady teams and coaches, but I'm not in a position to mentor them and disciple them. So, I was so grateful God brought an incredible teammate, Lindsay Rorick, to be our lead in Fort Worth, TX with all of our lady coaches and athletes. A huge answered prayer! Her faith and journey with God has really blessed and inspired me. Her voice is crucial to our city and I wanted her to share her journey in forgiveness with you.

> *I have had the opportunity to play sports most of my life. I played basketball in high school and on the collegiate level. In the sports world, there are many hard days of balancing school and social life while also working relentlessly to be the best athlete possible. I had a coach in high school who was extremely verbally abusive to me and my teammates. Having grown up as an athlete, the title "Coach" was one which gained immediate respect in my eyes. He knew the weight that his voice carried in my mind, and he used that power to tear me down. The way he spoke to me left me feeling scared, worthless, and unloved. For years, I held onto anger and resentment towards him. The demeaning words that he used to speak over me would play repeatedly in my mind. I allowed my compounding anger towards him to affect my perception of and relationship with other male leaders in my life.*
>
> *After years of holding onto this unhealthy resentment, I was having coffee with my close friend one day and she asked me, "What will it take for you to forgive him?" At the time, I was angry at her for even asking me that. I quickly replied, "He never once apologized to any of us for the way he spoke to us, so why should I forgive him?" to which she calmly whispered, "Your forgiveness isn't for him to earn, it's for you to be set free." (Not only can God speak to us through His*

Word, but God can speak through His people! Be open to those around you trying to speak into your life.) For me, it was a gamechanger.

She will never know the extent to which her words impacted me that day. She was right. I had been waiting around for him to earn the right to be forgiven, which is not even a part of the narrative of what forgiveness is all about. Forgiveness, I learned, is about extending mercy to those who hurt us—even when they don't deserve it. Choosing to forgive my coach did not excuse his actions or words towards me, but it released the power that they held over my life. During my journey of forgiveness, I was reminded that God extends this same mercy to us every single day. We have done nothing to earn or deserve His grace and even so, He loves us and forgives us anyway.

I am now in a place where I can acknowledge the hurtful words that were said by my coach, but not carry them around as unhealthy baggage. I can express the pain that his words caused me at that time, and in the same breath walk empowered knowing that those past words and actions no longer hold power over me. Finally, I can extend empathy and forgiveness to a coach who is a fallen, broken human just like me. Choosing forgiveness has allowed me more physical, emotional, mental, and spiritual freedom than I have ever known. I have gained more perspective for the Father's love for me and the grace that He gives His children. Thank You, Lord, for allowing the Holy Spirit to speak through my friend that day. Walking in forgiveness has been one of my sweetest gifts. Today, I get the honor to lead, mentor, and impact coaches and athletes through the platform of Fellowship of Christian Athletes.

If you have unforgiveness, I want to ask you the same question my friend asked me. What will it take for you to forgive ___________? You deserve to be free. Do not waste another minute carrying something God wants to bury! Freedom is waiting." ➧

9

TAKE YOUR PLACE

Charles Woodson was one of my favorite football players to watch. He won the Heisman trophy in college and became a Hall of Fame player in the NFL. For a few years, I was lucky enough to see him up close as I had the opportunity to work with the Oakland Raiders. One thing that blew me away about Charles was that he wasn't the fastest athlete on the field, nor was he the strongest. In fact, he probably wasn't even the most talented player on the team. But none of that mattered. His work ethic and ability to be a great teammate made up for what he lacked. On top of that, I believe what made him one of the greatest playmakers in the league was his understanding of his position. Woodson had a way of always being in the *right position* at the *right time*. Whether it was a big interception, a fumble recovery, a strip-sack on the quarterback, or a huge deflection—he was always in the right spot to make a big play.

Do you know that this principle works the same way, spiritually? Maybe you're not destined to be a Hall of Famer. That's okay. Very few are. You still have a position to play in the game of life. There are things that God has planned for you to do that will not be released until you are in the right position to receive them. God's blessings are always ready to be released over your life but cannot be until your heart is in position for Him to act according to His laws of redemption, healing, and deliverance. God is not withholding His blessings! The bottom line is, we need to be in position to receive them.

The Bible tells us of several instances where position made all the difference in the world. Let's look at a few examples:

Two women. Mary and Martha were two women in leadership who served in completely different capacities yet clearly understood their positions. One took her place at the feet of Jesus while the other was always busy doing things for Him.

A great city. Positioning made all the difference for Jesus' hometown of Nazareth. Once, He returned there to do miracles but could not because of their familiarity with Him. They just saw Him as the boy next door, not the Messiah. Jesus desired to heal the sick in the city, but the people weren't in a proper spiritual position to receive.

A future king. Positioning made all the difference when the future king, David, left his sheep to serve his brothers some lunch, who were—not-so-coincidentally—at war with Goliath. The rest is history.

A very sick woman. Positioning was the difference for a lady who suffered from a blood disorder. The crowd told her to stay away from Jesus, but she crossed the line to press into her miracle.

A Savior. Of course, the ultimate positioning was Jesus (God) leaving Heaven to position Himself as a man so the unseen God could now be seen. Jesus ultimately positioned Himself on the cross to pay for our sins by defeating death, hell, and the grave!

When God created the heavens and the earth, He caused a mist to rise from the ground to provide moisture for all the trees and plants. Look what the Bible says about it!

"These are the generations of the heavens and of the earth when they were created, in the day that the Lord God made the earth and heavens and every plant of the field before it was in the earth, and every herb of the field before it grew. For the Lord God had NOT caused it to RAIN upon the earth, and there was NOT a man to till the ground."[1]

Isn't it crazy to think that before then, no water had ever come DOWN? Rain, as we know it, had never fallen before this! It wasn't until Man—not just one man, but Mankind—was in position that God caused it to rain. Position was the key.

Maybe you're experiencing what seems to be a "mist" of blessings right now, but in your heart you know God has more for you. You know God wants to "rain" down on you. Why not stop and ask yourself, *Is God waiting on me to be in a different spiritual position before He pours out His rain on my life?*

Now, let me be clear of what that "rain" can be. Rain can come in the form of healing, wisdom, influence, or even an answer you've been waiting for. It could be an idea that will bless you and your family. It could be a new or better job, a great relationship, or even *the* relationship! More importantly, it can be hearing His voice and feeling His presence.

. . . You already have everything you need to be all that God desires you to be!

Remember, before God created Man, He first created everything Man needed. What does this mean for you? It means that you already have everything you need to be all that God desires. He's not looking for your abilities; He's looking for your availability. When you surrender your whole life to Him—choosing His ways over your ways—you, then, position yourself for God to pour down His rain of peace, self-control, joy, and so much more. It's not always easy, but it's worth it!

Your enemy could care less if you're the smartest, strongest, fastest, most talented, most creative, etc. All he desires is to get you out of God's position. Just like a defender in basketball tries to keep his opponent from setting up for his shot, the enemy is battling you for your position. His goal is to get into your head, steal the ball, and ultimately stop you.

It's time to know your position and stand up against your enemy!

FINDING YOUR PLACE

If you feel out of position right now, there are three things I see that can get you to where God desires you to be.

#1

BE PRAYED UP

Any athlete knows that before they can take their position on the team, they have to first receive direction from the coach. It's the same way with God. Before you can truly know your position and where you need to be at this time in your life, you have to know what "Coach God" says about it. And for that to happen, you have to connect with Him! Believe me, your enemy will try to distract you and block you every time you try to communicate with God or spend time with him. So, you have to be focused and make Him a priority—not just "a" priority, TOP priority! Remember, everything in your life flows out of this one relationship.

. . . Just know, you will never have time for God!

Straight up, just know, you will never have time for God! No one does. You have *make* time for Him. Throughout the years, people have asked me, "Chris, how do you balance ministry and family?" My answer is simple: "I don't believe in balance; I believe in priorities." In my life, it's always God first, then marriage, kids, and ministry. Everything else just has to get behind that. You see, when you make things a priority, it happens naturally.

Connecting with God primarily happens in prayer. Prayer is so powerful. In his book *Fresh Fire*, Pastor Jim Cymbala said, "I've seen God do more in people's lives during 10 minutes of real prayer than in 10 of my sermons." Prayer will build God's church, God's way! *(In the Appendix at the back of the book, you'll find "Quick Tips to Up Your Game in Prayer." It's a really simple prayer format using the acronym A.C.T.S. This is also the same prayer guide that helped me tremendously as a 19-year-old who didn't know squat about prayer. Go check it out!)*

Prayer moves the heart of God, and it ultimately changes our heart. Prayer is powerful, and it works. God wants to answer our prayers because it blesses (His children) and increases our faith! If you prayed and believed for someone to get healed and they did, wouldn't you naturally want to go pray for someone else? Absolutely you would!

One time, I was speaking to our young adults group in San Jose, CA. I'll never forget this night as long as I live. As I was wrapping up my message, I felt God speak to my heart that He wanted to do something miraculous if I would be willing to step out in faith. I could sense the presence of God in the room so strongly, so in my heart I was like, "Absolutely, Lord! For sure! I believe!"

Way in the back, there was a young adult visiting the service that night. He was a known active gang member in the area, but that's not what caught my attention about him. I noticed he wore hearing aids. So, as I'm speaking, I felt God nudge my heart, saying, "Tell him I want to heal him. Pray for his healing." Instantly, fear and doubt came over me like a tsunami! Even worse though, I started listening to the enemy's voice: *"You're just going to embarrass him!" What if God doesn't heal him! What if I make this guy mad and he comes after me!?"* All REAL thoughts and valid concerns. Yet, at the same time, I sensed God and my faith rising in my spirit.

Finally, I said, "We're going to pray together tonight and believe for people to experience God. I feel like some healings are going to happen." Then, I did it. I called on this young man and asked if I could pray for him. He nodded and said, "Yes." So, I asked everyone to join me in believing God to heal his hearing. In that moment, I felt the Holy Spirit directing me to take his hearing aids off and throw them away and that when I would do that, God would heal him. But I didn't listen and the voice of fear and doubt just started screaming in my head. Instead, I ended up praying and then asked him if he would be able to hear me if he took off his hearing aids, to which he said, "No." But, I asked if he would take them off anyways.

When he took them off, I stood behind him just praying my heart out to God to heal this guy. I prayed his life would never be the same. It seemed like I stood there praying FOREVER and nothing was happening. But then . . .

All of a sudden, he began to raise his hand slowly into the surrender posture. The audience started clapping and then they got louder and louder. Out of curiosity, I walked in front of him to see what was happening. As I did, I saw huge tears streaming down his face. I asked him quietly what was happening and he said, "I can hear you and hear everyone praying!" Quickly, I walked behind him again but this time stood back about five feet and prayed! I said, "If you can hear me, say, 'I love Jesus!'" He yelled, "I LOVE JESUS!" I said, "If you are healed and can hear me, say, 'Thank You for healing me!'" He yelled, "THANK YOU FOR HEALING ME!"

The entire room erupted, many wept and fell to their knees. It was truly a miracle!

That moment marked me for life. It changed me. Now, has God healed every person I've prayed for? No. Has He healed others since healing this young man? Yes. Do I know why He healed him and not others? No. My job is not to heal (because I couldn't heal anybody anyways). My job is only to be obedient to God and pray. When God moved and answered my prayer, it increased my faith and made me realize that I have to be bold in stepping out to pray for people every time I feel a nudge in my heart. There is power in prayer. I've seen it AND I've experienced it! It's real!

#2

BE PREPARED

Everybody wants to be the star, but do they want to do the preparation? The greatest athletes I've ever been around, like Tim Brown and Jerry Rice, spent countless hours preparing on and off the field. When it was time to shine, that's exactly what they did! Preparation was the key.

We need to learn how to control the "control-ables"—the things we can take personal ownership and responsibility for.

While spending time with God in prayer awaiting your position, keep sharpening your craft and gift. You never know when the door of opportunity will open, and you will have a window to walk through it.

Along with the athletes who have spent countless hours preparing when no one was watching, I've also, unfortunately, witnessed many who were not ready when their door of opportunity opened—and I'm not just talking about talent here. Some athletes' talent took them to the top, but they never prepared their character and *integrity* which caused them to miss their moment.

One of the most valuable lessons life has taught me is that there are a lot of things in life that we can't control. I can't count the number of people I've heard worry and complain about things they have no control over. We need to learn to control the "control-ables"—the things we can take personal ownership and responsibility for. Things like effort, mindset, attitude, and *preparation.* So, take what you can control and steward it well.

There's nothing quite like walking into class and hearing your teacher say, "Hey, we are having a pop test," and have total peace because you're prepared. Or, having your coach call your name off the bench, and you perform like a starter—because you were prepared!

So, where are you today? Are you an athlete who's killing it on the field but dropping the ball in class? Are you out of college seeking your calling and wondering what your next step will be? Wherever you are in life, prepare your heart. Prepare your mind. Prepare your spirit for the task ahead. Be prepared to the best of your ability.

#3

BE PATIENT

Right next to "preparation"—on the most-hated list of characteristics—is patience! But no matter how many times you hear, "Trust the process," it's true: You must trust *and enjoy* the process of development. Most importantly, trust God during the process. God sees what you don't see, and He knows things you don't know. You can rely on His character and track record. He is a good and faithful God who has never forsaken His people, . . . and He won't start with you!

Here's something to understand: God's main concern isn't your comfort but your character. His focus is on *who* you are becoming, not *what* you're becoming. The Bible says, *"Your word is a lamp to my feet and a light to my path."*[2] A lamp or lantern only shows your next step. I know we would all rather use a big floodlight to see the whole picture, but many times God only shows us the next few steps. Why? Because He wants us to trust him and walk in faith, and He wants to walk with us every step of the way! If He showed us everything at once, our tendency might be to say, "Thanks, God, but. I got it from here!" and that would not be a good thing.

When I stepped down from my pastor position in San Jose, CA to answer God's calling for my family to move to Texas, I only knew a few things. I knew we were supposed to move to the Dallas/Fort Worth area, and I knew the church where we were to serve. Immediately, my lightning-fast mind was like, "Ohhh, I see what You're doing, God! My next step is moving to Texas and going on staff at this mega-church! Man, this stepping out in faith stuff is pretty easy."

Well, I had half of it right!

When we got to Texas, we started attending this mega-church and it was incredible! The presence of God, the amazing staff, amazing teaching, amazing worship, incredible children and youth programs—it was awesome! I started building relationships quickly, all the while thinking, *Here we go! I'll be hired any day now.*

Didn't happen! In fact, the exact opposite.

When push came to shove, financially, I started working at Costco and driving a school bus. You talk about humbling! People would call me and ask, "What are you doing? Did you leave your position in Cali to work at Costco in Texas? Are you crazy?" Friends, family—they all wrote me off. I even started to doubt myself. But what I didn't see was how God was working behind the scenes.

We had young kids at the time, and I needed to find a job that provided insurance for my family. Through some mutual friends, I ended up connecting with the Fellowship of Christian Athletes (FCA) in the Dallas area. During the interview and hiring process, the only thing I could think was, *This is just a season. As soon as the church hires me, I'm out.* As time went on, I came to realize that trusting God and raising funds was much harder than I ever expected.

It came to the point where my wife and I were so broke and frustrated that she yelled out, "Why won't the church just hire you?!" At that moment, I felt the Holy Spirit speak to me and say, "That's not the right question. The right question is 'Why have I not opened that door?'" That hit me hard, but at the same time I was relieved and peace came over us. At that moment, we knew God had the power to open whatever door He desired and for reasons we didn't understand at the time, He deemed it best to not open that one.

A few months later, the church had to make a tough decision to lay off about one-third of their staff! Now, what if I would have left FCA to join the church staff, only to be laid off within a few months? God knew! Learning the power of patience is so powerful.

Everybody wants "flashlight" living, but God works on "lamp" living—one step at a time with Him. Do you want to know your position? Then let Him guide you. The Bible says, *"Rejoice in hope, be patient in tribulation, be constant in prayer."*[3] I heard it best put this way: "Patience is not the ability to wait; it's the ability to keep a good attitude while waiting!"

Pray.

Prepare.

Be patient.

God has your perfect position carved out just waiting for you!

10

THE POWER OF VISION

I was standing in front of about 30 high school students one day, teaching them how to find purpose in life. In the middle of my presentation, I put a picture of a brand new Ferrari on the screen. Then, I asked this question, "Describe to me what type of person owns and drives this car?" One kid answered, "A doctor or a lawyer." Another said, "A social media influencer, like a YouTuber." One other said, "A hip hop star." Was there a correct answer to this question? No, not at all. The whole exercise wasn't for them to see the car, but rather to see *how* they saw it. It proved my point then and now: *How we see life affects every aspect of our lives.*

Vision is powerful. A recent survey asked 1,000 people across America, "If you could have only one of your five senses, which one would it be?"[1] The leading answer? Vision. Some would say that sight and vision are the same. I disagree. I've always defined the two as: *Sight* is seeing through our eyes; *vision* is seeing through

God's eyes. Knowing these two distinct definitions, let me now ask you two very important questions:

- What are you seeing?
- What can be seen through your life?

In biblical times, whatever people saw and how they saw things literally meant life or death for many. One story in the Old Testament tells us how God commanded this gentleman and his wife to leave a city.[2] Not only did God tell them to leave, but He specifically told them to never look back. For whatever reason, as they were leaving the city, this man's wife disobeyed God's instructions and turned her head for one last look. When she looked back, she immediately turned into a pillar of salt! (This story always reminds me of when I drive by an accident on the freeway, and the "rubberneckers" all slow down to gawk instead of just normally driving by—making the rest of us behind them come to a slow crawl! Man, I get so mad, . . . and then I go and do the exact same thing! Ha!

Sight is seeing through our eyes; vision is seeing through God's eyes.

Just what is it about us having to see it for ourselves? I don't know what it is, but we all sure do it!

Another story of the power of vision is when King David saw a young woman bathing one day.[3] One glimpse led him down a series of making some really bad choices which ended with him having her husband murdered just to cover up his sin.

Another example is the two thieves who were hanging next to Jesus on the cross.[4] One saw Jesus as someone who could get them out of their current situation. The Bible says he yelled at Jesus and said, "So, You're the Messiah, are You? Prove it by saving Yourself and us!" The other thief saw Jesus a little differently. He cried out to his friend, the other thief, and said, "Do you not even fear God, even when you are sentenced to die? We deserve to die for our crimes, but this Man hasn't done anything wrong!" Then, he turned to Jesus and said, "Jesus, remember me when you enter Your kingdom." Jesus replied, "I assure you, today you will be with Me in paradise." Wow!

Two thieves in the same situation but with two very different visions. The point is clear: Where you focus your eyes is where you will go. Some tend to keep their eyes on their past, and they keep going in circles. One of my coaches once told me, "There's a reason that a car's windshield is huge, and the rearview mirror is small. Keep your eyes looking ahead, Son." That's a timeless truth. Don't focus on your past but keep your eyes on what's in front of you.

Where you focus your eyes is where you will go.

Some people can't help but to look to their right or left, constantly comparing themselves to what everyone else is doing. On the other hand, other people only look at themselves all the time. Let me encourage you to keep your eyes off of the past, off of others, and even off of yourself! Keep your eyes on Jesus.

God's Word says it best:

". . . but I focus on this one thing; forgetting the past and looking forward to what lies ahead, I press on to reach the end of the race and receive the heavenly prize for which God, through Christ Jesus is calling us."[5]

WHAT DO THEY SEE?

What you see is important, but what others see in you is also extremely valuable. In athletics, in family, and in the workplace, what can be seen *through* your life will have a huge impact on you and others. First of all, you may be the only Jesus someone will ever see! People who are constantly around you may never step foot in a church to hear a preacher.

What do they see in you?

If you're not sure how to answer that question, ask yourself these ones first:

- *Does your life challenge people to work hard?*
- *Does it encourage people to want to pursue God?*
- *Are you a blessing to others?*
- *Do you encourage those around you to take the easy road?*
- *Are you leading people down the wrong road?*
- *How will your friends remember you?*

A friend of mine's family purchased a beach condo close to Santa Cruz, CA some years ago. He told me it was a two bedroom, two bath, 989 square feet condo, which they paid 1.9 million dollars for! I was blown away. When I finally had a chance to visit, we pulled up to this older home. Honestly, there really wasn't anything special about it. I walked inside and the first thing I thought was, *Man, this doesn't feel like a two-million dollar place!* I'm thinking a house that cost that much would be some huge, lavish, baller-status house. I must've have had a look of disappointment on my face, because my friend walked me over to the living room and said, "This is why."

He then opened the curtains to the most awesome view of the Pacific Ocean! There it was right there in front of my eyes, and it was amazing! We opened the door and literally walked down a few steps onto the beach.

When we view life through God's eyes, people begin to see how life should and could be lived . . .

I learned that day how real estate values increase or decrease depending on one very important thing: the view! The same principle applies in life, as well.

What people see in our lives makes a *huge* impact. The main goal is that people see Jesus in us. How is that accomplished? By the life, love, and character of Jesus Christ being on full display in our actions, attitudes, behavior, and words. When we view life through God's eyes, people begin to see how life should and could be lived—selfless, generously, loving, honorable, and more. When we start representing Christ in everything we do and say, then we will start to see real change in racism, violence, broken homes, etc. It starts with us—the people who have encountered God!

Remember, *sight* is what you see through your eyes; *vision* is what you see through God's eyes.

And Jesus should be what people see in you!

So, the question is, "What are people seeing in your life right now?" I dare you to ask an adult who knows you, "What do you see when you see my life?" Ask a coach, a teacher, or a mentor. Be prepared to gain some valuable perspective. I promise that you'll start to have a new vision for life.

11

PEACE OUT

My heart is always saddened when I hear about celebrities who die from tragic situations. I remember famous singer Amy Winehouse's death years ago. Any death at that age is a sad thing, but especially when you see someone searching and struggling through life. It reminds me of one of my favorite movie quotes from *A Bronx Tale* that says, "The saddest thing in the world is wasted talent." Amy used her talent and gifting but for whatever reason, made certain choices to use drugs. It brings truth to the saying "Whenever you use drugs, drugs will always use you."

When the news of Amy's death began to surface, so many people were tweeting and posting, "R.I.P." This phrase had me pondering all day. Rest in peace? I know people meant well, but what does this really mean? Do people really know what they're saying? What is peace? How do you know you—or better yet, the ones who have passed—have it? Do they know what happens after death? Do they believe in the Heaven and Hell that the Bible teaches? Or do they believe everyone goes to Heaven and just gets to rest in peace?

The week that Amy passed was one of the toughest weeks of my life. Another death happened that week which gained no media attention. It was that death where I learned what true peace really is.

My wife was 12 weeks pregnant, and we had the typical 12-week doctor checkup. I woke up excited and ready for the day, having no idea my life would change forever.

The previous three days had been a crazy roller coaster ride—one I would never wish anyone to experience. Now, it was time to hear our baby's heartbeat, once again. As we sat in that doctor's office on that Tuesday afternoon, my life changed forever. It was then that we were told that our baby's heart had stopped beating a week before our appointment.

> **Peace has *nothing* to do with the absence of fear but *everything* to do with the presence of Christ and His Holy Spirit.**

Our first baby. Our dream. Our little bean we had fallen in love with, now was gone . . . forever. The next 48 hours were full of prayer, tears, and more tears. It felt like we were in a washing machine being tossed around by anger, hurt, confusion, and shock. In our minds, our baby had been taken from us, and we had no time to deal with it. The next day, we were pushed from office to office, from waiting room to waiting room. Finally, the day ended with my wife having one of the most painful procedures anyone could ever imagine. Our lifeless baby was taken out of her womb.

Being a minister, I have preached about faith and peace many times, but both seemed so foreign in that moment . . . and yet, more real than ever. So, it brought me to this question: "What is real peace?"

THE REAL PEACE

When most people think of peace, they think "calm conditions." We associate peace way differently than God does. Peace has *nothing* to do with the absence of fear but *everything* to do with the presence of Christ and His Holy Spirit. We see this when Jesus appeared to His disciples after the resurrection:

> *"While they were still talking about this, Jesus himself stood among them and said to them, 'Peace be with you.' They were startled and frightened, thinking they saw a ghost."*[1]

Notice that before Jesus pronounced peace, He (the Prince of Peace) was already with them in the room. Peace was embodied *with* them in the midst of their circumstances. What people mostly desire is calm conditions, not peace. The truth is, God never promised calm conditions! But He did promise His *presence* . . . which is His *peace*! Jesus said it this way:

> *"And surely I am with you always, to the very end of the age."*[2]

. . . anytime you have to step out in faith, you will always have to step over fear.

For me and Kristina, during that particular week, it was God's *presence* that filled us with *peace* during our most un-peaceful circumstance. You see, peace isn't found in a positive doctor's report. Peace isn't the absence of any trials or conflict in your home life or marriage. Having a ton of money can't bring you real peace. Peace isn't even knowing what the future holds for your life.

What is true peace?

True peace is knowing the fact that Jesus Christ and His Holy Spirit are with you even when you get a bad doctor's report. That Jesus Christ is with you in those tough times at home. That He is with you now and with you forever in your future. Remember what Jesus said, "Peace be *with* you." He was saying, "I am peace, and when I'm with you, you can have peace!"

MOVE IT OR CLIMB IT

That week taught me a very important lesson: God brings His peace into situations where fear is the strongest and when we're the most frightened. I heard one pastor say it like this: "It's in the moments when we need God's peace most desperately that He supplies it most abundantly." As much as my wife and I desired calm conditions, we instead found God's presence and true peace in the midst of chaos.

Have you ever noticed that when faced with the mountains

of hurt, debt, illness, fear, etc., most of the time we just want the mountain to leave? And wouldn't it be great! But the reality is this: Sometimes God moves the mountains; other times, He gives us the strength and courage to climb it! Don't be afraid to scale up that mountain and take it. Remember, anytime you have to step *out* in faith, you will always have to step *over* fear.

Sometimes God moves the mountain; other times, He gives us the strength and courage to climb it!

I can't imagine going through tragic moments without the presence of God and His peace—and we have had our fair share, believe me. Since the time of losing our first baby, my wife has suffered three more miscarriages. But, we rode out the storm. In the end, God blessed us with three miracle children! We often tell people that we have seven kids—four in Heaven praying and cheering us on and the other three here on earth. One day, we will be reunited in God's presence. But for now, my mom is enjoying them in God's presence as we continue to go after the mission God has for us here on earth.

Today, you might be wondering why you've gone through what you have and why life hurts at times. Whatever storm you're facing today—whether it be the divorce of your parents, an injury, fear of what's happening in our world, or dealing with rejection—this I can promise you: Everyone faces difficulties. There's something else I can promise you: Not everyone comes through the storms of life. Some drown in the storm. How do you survive the storm? Get Jesus in your boat *right now*!

The Bible says, "Now is the day for salvation."[3] Don't wait. When Jesus is in your boat—in other words, in your heart and in your life—the storms will still come but your boat will not sink! You will get through it, and God will shine through you. How do I know? Because the tomb is empty. He rose from the dead, proving He was who He said He was, the everlasting God. What this means is that you can trust His Word and His promises.

12

NOW, RUN!

The Bible describes our journey here on earth in many different ways, but the one I like best is a race. Near the end of his life, the Apostle Paul writes to his protégé and says:

> *"I have fought the good fight, I have finished the race, and I have remained faithful."* [1]

The Bible even talks about a crowd of people who have gone before us and are cheering us on from the grandstands of Heaven. As they cheer, we can run our race with endurance, keeping our eyes on Jesus as we do. If you thought the Oakland Raiders had crazy fans, I bet these guys make Raider Nation look tame in comparison! And they're cheering for you AND me!

I like to look at our journey here on earth as a relay race. My favorite Olympic race is the 4 x 100 relay. It's fast, intense, and I love that it involves precision teamwork. Someone starts and does their best to stay in their lane and run with everything they have. Then, they must pass the baton—seamlessly—to the second runner. Sometimes, that person is in last place, but they have the ability to catch up during their leg of the race. Then, the third runner receives the baton, and finally, the last one finishes the race.

To me, the greatest part about this race is watching the runners take over where their teammates left off. They all build upon each other's performances. Maybe I love it so much because it sounds just like the race of life!

Do you know who those people in Heaven's grandstand are? They are the Bible greats who ran the race before you. Reading their stories in the Bible not only teaches you how to run, but also provides encouragement and equipping for you to run your own race.

Think about it this way. There was a generation who did great things for God like start churches and campus clubs. Now, they are passing that baton *to you*! Their part of the race has helped establish where you begin. The great thing is that it doesn't matter if they gave you the baton in last place. You can change it! When you start running with everything that's in you, you know that your stride matters to impact your generation. Then, guess what?

You get to hand off that baton to the generation coming behind you!

PASS THE BATON

I have to say that the baton handed to me wasn't the best. I grew up in a broken home and never had much. We were so poor that we had to eat at family's and friends' homes on certain days of the week. I never could afford a pair of Jordans. As a matter of fact, my Adidas sneakers had four stripes instead of three! (Yes, they were knock offs!) We couldn't afford Lucky Charms, so we bought Lucky Stars! When I say, "Poor," I mean it.

Worse than the lack of money, my family tree was filled with divorce, alcohol, and drug abuse. To make things worse, my mom was diagnosed with cancer and died when I was 11 years old. I was then adopted by my grandparents and moved to San Jose, CA.

This was the baton handed to me.

I never had any idea of this race until June 22, 1997. That's the day I decided to give my life to Christ. That day, I realized that my race mattered, so I started running it with everything inside of me. Today, I'm celebrating 12 years of marriage to my wife Kristina. We have three miracle children who will never have to wonder if Daddy is coming home or if there's food in the fridge. Every day they will be hugged, kissed, prayed over, and told, "I love you!"—and my race is just getting started.

BETWEEN THE LINES

That's my story, but what about yours? Have you started your race? What baton was given to you? No matter where you started, you can do this! You need to run like people's lives are on the line. Why? Because they are!

Whatever you do, don't run alone. Find mentors and get them in your life. Be careful who you surround yourself with. Remember, whoever you connect with today will change the stories you tell tomorrow.

Remember, whoever you connect with today will change the stories you tell tomorrow.

There are two things I want to encourage you with concerning this race called life, and I want to use an example from a track. When runners set up in their lane, they put themselves between a line on their left and a line on their right. That lane is what guides them in the race and helps them not crossover to someone else's lane. For your race, these two lines represent your two purposes on this planet—your *universal* purpose and your *unique* purpose.

Let's take a look at both.

LINE#1

UNIVERSAL PURPOSE

Your universal purpose in this life is to know Christ and to become like Him in your heart. You're called to seek Him and put Him first in all things.

Every single one of us is called to be like Jesus and to become like Jesus. The Bible helps us see a clear picture of who God is and what He is like. It shows how Jesus loved the less fortunate, served all people, and how religious people frustrated and angered Him. We see His patience, His love, His faith, and His compassion for all people. That's the life we are all called to live—to walk like Jesus in His behavior, mindset, choices, and character.

Just think what this world would look like if every Believer lived like Him on a daily basis? You may be one of the many who are asking, "What is God calling me to do?" or, "Where am I supposed to be in the next five years?" Those are great questions, but not necessarily the right ones! I've learned that when you begin to focus on the *known* will of God, He begins to reveal His *unknown* will. Don't focus on the unknown; instead, focus on what's right in front of you—the known.

It's all laid out in the Bible. I've had many people ask me questions like, "How did you become a sports chaplain? How did you start helping professional football teams? How did you connect with pro boxers? In my college years, I dreamt of being on big stages and speaking at packed out events, but what I learned was to follow Him one day at a time and to be obedient to what He said and where He led me. I wasn't chasing man's approval or the crowd; I was chasing God—and the whole time God was leading me.

. . . when you begin to focus on the *known* will of God, He begins to reveal His *unknown* will.

One day, I was with my mentor and read in the newspaper where Napoleon Kaufman, the number one pick for the Oakland Raiders that year, was going to be at a mall in the area. I told my mentor, "Let's drive over there and meet him. I heard he loves the Lord." We went over, bought a ticket for an autograph, and met him. We didn't waste any time sharing our passion for God! Napoleon was blown away! Then, I asked him, "Do you want to impact young people?" From there I started meeting with him and quickly became friends. Then, BOOM, ministry began. From there, I started serving pro football, baseball, and basketball teams; pro boxers, and more.

You see, God is working all around you, right now. As you pursue Him, He will reveal where He's working and will invite you to be a part. The rest is history.

Your greatest purpose in life is this: *to pursue His presence and come to know God.* Make His presence a *priority* and your *passion*; He'll do the rest. You'll start finding peace in being obedient to Him and peace in who you are—His child.

LINE #2

UNIQUE PURPOSE

The second line that makes up your lane is your unique purpose—the thing God had reserved for you to do like no one else on the planet! Whether it's being a pastor, musician, writer, teacher, doctor, athlete, or director, there is something just for you that *only you* can fulfill.

Your mission won't look like anyone else's. The

world needs *you* to be *you*! We don't need another Billy Graham, Michael Jordan, Tom Brady, or Jeff Bezos. No, we need you! You are gifted and talented; and with God, you will have a great impact in the lane God calls you to run in.

I have a friend who is the lead singer for a music group called All-4-One. In the 1990s, that band sold over 20 million records! Huge success. The group met in their church in Southern California, and they loved singing clean love songs. Of course, not everybody, especially some Christian leaders, was excited about his career. In fact, many of them said things like, "You can't keep singing for the world. You need to do Gospel music!" They quoted many scriptures to back their case, so he decided, "Well, I guess I need to do Gospel music." So he did, and it was an incredible album!

As my friend, did his best to sing in churches across America, God kept putting people on his heart—specific people: people who would never step foot in a church. He called me one day and said, "Chris, I'm frustrated. I feel God is calling me to be a light in dark places." I agreed with him. It was evident.

God's hand and favor have always been on his life, and it continued in his new role. It was so normal for me to be hanging out with him and his family and for him to receive texts or calls from some of the music industry's biggest stars asking for prayer or wanting to come by and see him and his family. Today, he gets to be a light to some of the biggest influencers in Hollywood—people that most preachers will never get access to.

Everyone has a specific and unique calling, and we hurt as a team when one person is out of position! Look at how the Bible says it:

> *"The human body has many parts, but the many parts make up one whole body. So it is with the body of Christ. . . .Yes, the body has many different parts, not just one part . . . But our bodies have many parts, and God has put each part just where he wants it. How strange a body would be if it had only one part! Yes, there are many parts, but only one body."*[2]

The fight for this generation is one where we need an army to rise up together. We need an army that understands its roles and positions. An army that will fight for more than just themselves. You are part of this army! Your life matters. You are important in this story called life. So, rise up. Don't waste another second of your precious life!

TIME TO RUN

If you're looking for a sign from God, *this is it*! I can't promise that God will live up to all your expectations, but I can promise He will live up to His Word that says He will be with you, that you are *more* than a conqueror, that no weapon formed against you will prosper, and that you are chosen. So, run! Run with confidence that God is with you.

As you run your race, know that I'm praying for you and rooting for you. Your journey in this broken world will have tough times and tough moments—moments where you will feel like giving up and throwing in the towel. My prayer for you is the same as Jesus' prayer for Peter:

> *"I have prayed for you, Simon, that your faith may not fail. And when you have turned back, strengthen your brothers."*[3]

Basically, Jesus is telling Peter, "You are going to fail me, but when you do, don't lose your faith! And when you get back up, go and help out your brothers!" That is so powerful. He didn't say, "I can't believe you're going to fail Me. I prayed that you would be perfect."

I charge you with the same today. In all the hell you may face, *don't lose your faith.* Keep getting up. Don't quit. You're a Culture Changer. That's what we do. Let your life be like the Apostle Paul when he wrote:

> *"I press on to reach the end of the race and receive the heavenly prize for which God, through Christ Jesus, is calling us!"*[4]

This is it. You're chosen. Tomorrow is not promised. Today you have a chance and a choice. Here's the baton, now, run! Our fearful dark world is waiting. God is sending a faith-filled, fearless team to finish this thing out. Let's go.

One LOVE. One GOD. One WAY.

ABOUT THE AUTHOR
Chris Avila

Chris is passionate in his devotion to Jesus Christ. He's had the privilege of traveling the world as a pro sports chaplain, pastor, and motivational speaker to over 350,000 youth. Chris has been helping people connect with God for over 20 years. His relevant and down-to-earth teaching style has made him a sought-after speaker for camps, churches, and conferences and by pro athletes, entertainers, and coaches. His mission is to impact and inspire this generation to make ethical and moral choices throughout their lifetime based on Biblical truths to impact the culture.

Born in New Jersey, Chris grew up in a struggling family of three and learned the importance of having faith. Through many setbacks in life, especially losing his mother at the age of 12, Chris was determined to make something out of his life. Many doors opened for Chris early in his life. He worked for a major mainstream radio station, starred in an independent film and shot various commercials. At the age of 20, Chris felt the call of God and served on the chaplaincy team for the Oakland Raiders from 1999-2011. He continues to mentor and speak into the pro athlete community. In May 2002, Chris gained a bachelor's degree in Church Leadership at Bethany College in Scott's Valley California.

Currently, Chris resides in Ft. Worth, TX, where he works for Fellowship of Christian Athletes. He's a husband to his best friend and wife Kristina and a father to two gorgeous girls, Mayah and Aria, and son Diego.

CONTACT

If you would like to schedule Chris to come and speak at your event, conference, or special service or if you would like Chris to begin working with your players and/or coaches, he would love to speak to you. You can reach out to him through his website or social media.

Social Media

@mrchrisavila

Website

www.officialchrisavila.com

APPENDIX

Appendix

THE CALL THAT COUNTS

Many times in a game, especially in the last two minutes of it, there are referee calls that determine whether one team wins and one team loses. Those calls can sometimes win or lose championships, help to win college scholarships, influence the ranking of a potential draft pick, or increase the dollar amount of fan merchandise sold with a particular professional player's name on it. Those calls are important, but there's one call that's more important than any call made on the field or on the court—and that's the call you made to accept Christ as the Lord of your life. Regardless of what your sports career holds, making the decision to follow Christ makes you a winner in life and a winner in eternity. It doesn't mean you're better than everybody else; it means that no matter what you go through in your life, you can know that He will never leave you or forsake you. You will never be alone again.

If you have read this whole book or even just a few pages and you can't say that you know for sure if you have ever made the only call that matters—to accept Christ—you can do that right now by praying this simple prayer. Just read it out loud and mean it from the bottom of your heart. God hears you and knows right where you are. Are you ready? You can do this!

> "Jesus, I realize my ways fall short from Yours. My ways don't work and they separate me from You. I know I don't have all the answers, but I believe You died on the cross to pay for all my shortcomings and wrong decisions—not just today or yesterday but even for all that

will come. I believe You died for me AND rose again three days later, proving that You are God. Come into my heart right now. Help me to live for You all the days of my life. Today, I am forgiven and now carry PEACE with me wherever I go. Thank You, Jesus, that I get to spend eternity in Heaven with You because of Your gift on the cross. AMEN."

Mark this day DOWN! In fact, mark it down right here! This is your spiritual birthday!

My Spiritual Birthday

I encourage you to even celebrate it every year and remember the goodness of our God. In the book of John, Jesus tells us we have to be "born again," and if you prayed that prayer for the first time with all your heart, that's exactly what happened. You will never be the same! You will start to have new vision for life. Sight is what you see through your eyes, but VISION is what you see through God's eyes!

Now, two really important things!

First, follow up that life-changing call with some action! Start reading your Bible every day to help you grow stronger in your faith and stronger as a new Believer. If you don't have one, ask you spiritual mentor. They can get one for you. You can also go on my website (www.officialchrisavila.com) and find some resources that will help you grow in your daily Christian walk.

Second, get connected to a local community of Believers, the church. Don't get frustrated. Sometimes it takes a minute to find the right one, but keep looking and ask God to help you find the right place for you! He will, too! The people in your church become your teammates. They will help you grow and help you stay accountable. Remember, going to church won't make you a Christian, won't turn you into a saint, and won't even keep you from making wrong decisions. But, you'll find that the messages you hear when you go to church each week are just exactly the things you needed to hear/know to help you get through the next week. God's pretty cool that way! So, get connected and STAY connected!

QUICK TIPS TO UP YOUR GAME IN PRAYER

A.C.T.S.

Adoration. Yeah, I know, it's a churchy word, but just move past that for a second. It just means when you begin your prayer time, begin by honoring Him. Acknowledge who He is—that He is faithful, He is holy, He is a good Father, He is able to do all things . . . You get where I'm going with this? Just spend a few moments telling Him you love Him. This first part is about Him, not you. It's about reminding yourself how amazing He really is.

Confession. (Another churchy word, but it sticks.) This is your time to ask God for forgiveness in areas where you've fallen short or have just made mistakes—things like, "God, I'm sorry for losing my temper," or "Lord, forgive me for not being obedient to what You asked." Take this time to realize you are not perfect, but acknowledge your need for Him in your life and for the forgiveness He offers everyday.

Thanksgiving. Begin to thank Him for your blessings and the things that have been happening in your life—and be specific. Thank Him for answering prayer, thank Him for your marriage, your kids, your home, your health, your family, and your job. Thank Him for ways He's shown up big in your life and even for the small things He's done in your day today. *"God, thank You* *that my meeting went well." "Thank You for that gift from my mom." "Thank you for protecting us in that accident we were in."* You get the point? There are no certain things you have to say. Just thank Him for whatever is in your heart.

Supplication. This is where you tell God what you need in your life, things you are asking God to do for you, your family, or anyone you are praying for.

RESOURCES

Look, I cannot finish this book without offering you as much REAL help in your journey as possible. Check out these two resources that be a strength to you when you need it most and will up your game in your daily walk with God

If you need prayer right now or maybe you have questions about God, faith—or whatever, you need to log onto:

www.whenlifehurts.com

Click on "Chat with a Coach." This is an incredible FREE resource that has 24-hour availability, with people who truly care to listen and pray with you. I actually get the privilege of being one of those volunteer coaches who serve real people like you every week.

If you are a coach, athlete, or teacher, Fellowship of Christian Athletes is an incredible ministry that works on campuses all over the world to help engage, equip, and empower you to live for Christ and connect you with the local church. Go to:

www.fca.org

Look up your local rep who would love to help you.

ENDNOTES

1 - FULL OF IT

1. Matthew 6:11 (NIV)
2. Matthew 4:4
3. Psalms 119:105
4. Hebrews 4:12
5. Matthew 24:35 (KJV)
6. James 1:22 (ESV)
7. Matthew 5:6

2 - THE STORM

1. "California Gurls" by Katy Perry feat. Snoop Dogg
2. https://counterculturemom.com/mtvs-bob-pittman-says-he-owns-our-kids/
3. Ephesians 6:12 (NIV)

3 - CULTURE CHANGES

1. 2 Corinthians 5:15-21

4 - THE BATTLE FOR IDENTITY

1. Genesis 1:27
2. Matthew 16:13-16 (NIV)
3. Psalm 139:13-16 (NIV)

5 - THE BATTLE FOR PURITY

1. Psalm 119:9-11 (NLT)
2. Psalms 63:1

3. Romans 13:11-14
4. 1 John 1:9 (NIV)
5. James 5:16a (NIV)

6 - THE BATTLE FOR YOUR GIFTS

1. Exodus 4:1-3 (NLT)
2. 1 Thessalonians 5:16-18 (NLT)

7 - THE BATTLE FOR APPROVAL

1. Galatians 1:10 (NIV)
2. John 3:16
3. Ephesians 3:20

8 - THE BATTLE FOR FORGIVENESS

1. Matthew 6:14-15 (NIV)

9 - TAKE YOUR PLACE

1. Genesis 2:4-5
2. Psalms 119:105 (NASB)
3. Romans 12:12 (ESV)

10 - THE POWER OF VISION

1. https://today.yougov.com/topics/health/articles-reports/2018/07/25/five-senses-majority-would-miss-sight-most?fbclid=IwAR36bZ6-opjuWnoPPquntPNZ1mO0A9CH7NdETUge_JG-Vu22uipO_DD1pQ0
2. See Genesis 19.
3. See 2 Samuel 11.

4. See Luke 23:32-43.
5. Philippians 3:13b-14 (NLT)

11 - PEACE OUT

1 Luke 24:36-37 (NIV)

2 Matthew 28:20b (NIV)

3 2 Corinthians 6:2b

12 - NOW, RUN!

1. 2 Timothy 4:7 (NLT)
2. 1 Corinthians 12:12,14,18-20 (NLT)
3. Luke 22:32-33 (NIV)
4. Philippians 3:14 (NLT)